START WITH A
Vegetable

START WITH A
Vegetable

More Than 100 Easy, Tasty, Plant-Forward Recipes for Everyone

JESSICA SMITH

Countryman Press

An Imprint of W. W. Norton & Company
Independent Publishers Since 1923

Pages viii, 256: Anna Petrow; pages 14, 82, 117: iStock / Iana Kotova; pages 30, 63, 99, 131, 145, 175: iStock / vector_ann; page 49: iStock / kameshkova; page 162: iStock / Judy Unger; pages 188, 203 (kale): iStock / Daria Ustiugova; page 203 (spinach): iStock / Kassiia Sergacheva

For information about permission to reproduce selections from this book, write to Permissions, Countryman Press, 500 Fifth Avenue, New York, NY 10110

For information about special discounts for bulk purchases, please contact W. W. Norton Special Sales at specialsales@wwnorton.com or 800-233-4830

Manufacturing by Toppan Leefung Pte. Ltd.
Book design by Allison Chi
Production manager: Devon Zahn

Countryman Press
www.countrymanpress.com

An imprint of W. W. Norton & Company, Inc.
500 Fifth Avenue, New York, NY 10110
www.wwnorton.com

978-1-68268-883-0

10 9 8 7 6 5 4 3 2 1

For Frank,
forever

Contents

Introduction

THIS COOKBOOK IS A LOVE LETTER TO EVERYDAY VEGETABLES: love for the broccoli you grabbed as you raced through the produce aisle, that pound of tomatoes from the farmers' market, a bag of carrots hiding somewhere in the back of your fridge. Everyday vegetables constitute the lifeblood of home kitchens. They play an even more important role in dinner. Increasingly I hear people casually mention that they're trying to eat more plants. Maybe that includes you. The reasons to eat more plants are becoming hard to overlook, whether for personal health or the health of the planet.

While writing this book, my own reasons for eating more plants came into focus. First, it saves money. Ingredients for the Cauliflower Steak Frites with Muhammara (page 79), for example, cost a lot less than the Sheet-Pan Corn and Shrimp Bake (page 121). Second, eating vegetables is convenient. Many vegetarian sources of protein have long shelf lives. Some of them may be waiting for you, tucked away in your pantry, at this very moment. Check out the Plant Proteins chapter (pages 1–13) for even more ideas than what you already might have on hand. Vegetables also inspire meals full of texture, color, and flavor. In the right configuration, those everyday vegetables can become beautiful, delicious, healthy meals.

Since 2010, much of my professional life and—my husband will tell you—a lot of my personal life have revolved around thinking about recipes. Those recipes appear on my website, InquiringChef.com, and in the archives at CookSmarts.com, the meal planning company where I sharpened my recipe-writing skills. My brain always searches for ways to transform vegetables into meals accessible for busy home cooks, unique enough to keep it interesting at the dinner table, and appealing enough that my three kids might eat them—*might*. (Every food-loving parent should experience dinner-table pickiness from time-to-time. It keeps us humble.)

Maybe you want to eat more vegetables. Maybe you want to eat less meat. The best way to achieve either goal is to start with a vegetable. So in the pages of this book, you'll find more than 100 ways for vegetables to take center stage. The recipes are vegetable-forward but not entirely vegetarian. About a third of them include meat or fish, but for each of those, an easy variation can make the dish vegetarian, resulting in flexible recipes without a lot of extra effort.

Now let's get cooking!

Kitchen Cheat Sheet

SALT TO TASTE

Salt likely played an essential role in any delicious meal that you've eaten. Learning how to use it properly will help you love the food that you cook at home. Because salt matters as much as any other ingredient, you'll find specific measures in these recipes to help you get to the "right" amount. You still may want to add more, so always taste and adjust as you go. Trust yourself. You know what tastes good.

All the recipe testing for this book used Morton Coarse Kosher Salt, available at most grocery stores. If using table salt, reduce the amount listed by half. If using Diamond Crystal Kosher Salt, increase the given amount by 50 percent.

My pantry always contains a box of Maldon flaked sea salt, and yours should, too. Sprinkling it over finished vegetables adds a nice crunch and brings out even more flavor.

WHEN TO USE COOKING OIL VERSUS OLIVE OIL

Keeping it simple, this book primarily calls for using just two types of oil. Buy large bottles or containers of each and transfer portions into smaller containers with spouts to keep near the stove. Store the large containers in a cool, dark spot, and they'll last for a long time.

- Cooking oil has neutral flavor and a high smoke point. Use it to sear, roast, and make sauces whenever you don't want the oil to impart flavor or when using high heat. Avocado oil, which I like to use, has a high smoke point, around 520°F.
- Olive oil means extra virgin olive oil. Use it to sear, roast, and make sauces whenever you want to include its subtle, savory flavor and won't be using high heat. Olive oil has a lower smoke point, around 400°F, so don't use it in very hot pans.

Toasted sesame oil appears in a few recipes for sauces and stir-fry dishes. A little goes a long way, so buy it one small bottle at a time.

PARCHMENT PAPER IS YOUR FRIEND

When you roast food in the oven—such as, *ahem*, vegetables—sometimes it sticks, making cleanup a challenge. Parchment paper will help. Some of the recipes in this book don't call for parchment because the dish benefits from the caramelization that results from vegetables coming in contact with the hot pan. But you can line your baking sheet with parchment to minimize mess, even when a recipe doesn't say so.

Check the package of parchment paper for the recommended temperature limit, but keep in mind that, as long as it doesn't contact the heat source directly, such as when cooking pizza, you generally can use it safely at higher temperatures. Precut, compostable parchment sheets, which I like to use, can go right into the compost bin or pile with any food scraps.

USE FRESH CITRUS AND HERBS

Because these ingredients often appear last in a recipe, they can feel easy to skip, especially if you forgot them on your grocery run. But give them priority. Every time you shop, buy a lemon . . . and then use it! It takes almost no time to slice a lemon or lime and squeeze it on a dish, and fresh citrus often makes other tastes and flavors shine.

The same rule holds true for fresh herbs. A sprinkling of fresh herbs on a finished dish not only adds flavor, but it also makes the food look beautiful—and beautiful food is more fun to eat. In many recipes, common herbs can work interchangeably. If basil is expensive in winter, use cilantro. If you think cilantro tastes like soap, use parsley or rosemary. If you have a thriving basil plant, use the leaves on everything.

SHARPEN YOUR KNIVES

Most vegetables require cutting. Sawing through them with a dull knife can make anyone throw in the towel. If you don't feel comfortable sharpening knives yourself or don't have the right tools, research local places that offer the service and get it done. It doesn't cost as much as you might think, and it makes a huge difference.

TAKE SHORTCUTS

You don't need my permission to take shortcuts in the kitchen, but let's put it here just in case you forget. No one is grading you on how much effort you put into dinner. If jarred sauce, prechopped vegetables, store-bought pizza dough, or precooked frozen rice makes your life easier, use them.

Flavor Boosters

You can find all the ingredients for the recipes in this book at a well-stocked grocery store. Many of them may be sitting in your pantry or fridge already. The flavor boosters, however, might prove slightly less common in your kitchen. So here's a quick guide.

BREAD CRUMBS, specifically panko (or Japanese-style bread crumbs), run larger and taste lighter and flakier than traditional Italian-style bread crumbs. Crisp and crunchy, they work pure magic when toasted in butter and used to make Salerno Spaghetti with Broccolini (page 41) or Broccoli Caesar-ish Salad with Toasted Bread Crumbs (page 31).

COCONUT MILK means canned coconut milk, often shelved in the international aisle, and shouldn't be confused with the type sold cold as a dairy substitute. Each recipe specifies whether to use regular (full-fat) or light coconut milk.

CURRY PASTE comes in a variety of colors and serves as the foundation of many Thai dishes. Red curry paste offers more chili flavor, whereas green curry paste imparts more herbaceous notes. You can use them or other kinds interchangeably, but always adjust the amount to your spice tolerance. Don't forget to consider the source. Curry paste from Thailand will pack *much* more heat than American brands, such as Thai Kitchen. Taste before you cook and adjust as you go.

GOCHUJANG SAUCE, made from fermented red chile peppers, occurs commonly in Korean cooking. Look for one made with red chiles and other ingredients that might include garlic, soy sauce, sugar, or vinegar.

HARISSA PASTE, a hot sauce originated in Morocco, has smoky, savory flavors. An easily found brand, Mina Harissa comes in mild and spicy versions. The mild one has almost no heat but lots of flavor.

MISO PASTE, a traditional Japanese seasoning, comes primarily from soybeans. Much of the variety of colors and flavors results from the amount of time that it ages. The recipes in this book use shiro (white) miso. The grocery stores where I shop in Kansas City all carry the Miso Master brand, chilled, usually near the tofu.

PARMIGIANO-REGGIANO is a firm, aged Italian cheese, and its name is stamped on the rind. This book uses the shorter English word, *Parmesan*, but both terms mean "of or associated with the city of Parma." Measure it with your heart and save the rind! You can freeze the rind for months and use it to flavor the liquids for rice, pasta, and soups. You definitely will want to use it for Summer Squash Minestrone (page 105).

SOY SAUCE OR TAMARI, made from fermented soybeans, isn't just for Asian cooking anymore. Either one gives many dishes a rich, savory flavor. All the recipes in this book call for the low-sodium option because the flavor stretches further before becoming overly salty. Low-sodium tamari makes a good gluten-free option.

TAHINI, a thick, nutty, creamy paste, comes from ground sesame seeds. If you've had hummus, you've tasted tahini, which gives that dish its creamy texture and savory taste. Tahini separates while it sits, so give it a good stir before using. Look for the Soom brand.

How to Meal-Plan Like a Pro

Approach meal planning like a spectrum. At one end, you'll find people who cook multiple whole meals ahead of time and stock their fridge or freezer with them. At the opposite end, other people walk into the kitchen at 6 PM and wing it. At different times in your life, you'll gravitate toward one end of the spectrum or the other. But no matter where you may find yourself, a few points can make your time in the kitchen run more smoothly.

After nearly a decade as a professional meal planner (yes, an actual job) for Cook Smarts, I can see how the meal planning pieces fit together to save you time and money. Whether you're planning for two days or seven days of meals, the following tips will make the most of your time. The Cook Smarts team uses some of these same battlefield-tested tips to plan an entire *year* of meals . . . in one sitting!

DOUBLE UP

Whenever you roast a vegetable, cook a grain, make a sauce, or shake up a vinaigrette, double the batch. They all keep well in the fridge, and you can store them in the freezer for at least three months. (Sauces that contain dairy are one exception to the freezer rule because the freezer can change their texture.) Just make sure that you have a plan for round two, or they'll languish, unused. If you double up effectively, you'll have a collection of ingredients ready to go at the end of the week. These gems can make incredible lunches and easy dinners over the weekend. See No-Recipe Meals on page 254 for how mismatched leftovers can become some of your favorite meals.

PREP AHEAD

Even if you don't do a full session of meal prep ahead of time, look for a small moment in the day to prep one item so all the work isn't waiting for you at 6 PM. Chop a veggie, make a sauce, marinate some protein, or pull something from the freezer to thaw. You can knock out this quick task before cleaning up the dishes at night, while you drink your morning coffee, or during your lunch break. Having one item prepped and ready to go is the easiest way to talk yourself into making the dinner that you planned instead of ordering delivery. I speak from experience here.

BUY ONE HERB AT A TIME

It can prove hard to use an entire bunch of herbs in one week, so buy just one and use it all. Let's say you start the week with a bunch of cilantro. Use it up in tacos, burrito bowls, and a Thai salad. Then, in the following week, maybe change over to parsley to make Italian recipes. If you find yourself with an assortment of partially used fresh herbs, throw them all into a batch of Green Goddess Sauce (page 245) for salads, grain bowls, and dipping veggies.

COOK PERISHABLES FIRST

Yes, this advice seems obvious. But it's easy to forget food stashed in the back of the fridge. If you bought ingredients that will go bad quickly, cook and eat those first. If you bought salmon, for example, make the salmon meal before you consider anything else. The same goes for other seafood and meats and the perfect produce from the farmers' market—which won't stay perfect for long! The recipes in this book contain lots of protein possibilities and ideas for leftovers that you can assemble after you've eaten what won't last.

PLAN EASY WINS FOR BUSY NIGHTS

One or two nights of each week always seem to pose a challenge. Maybe your Monday nights are rough or the nights you have to work late or the kids have back-to-back activities. Whatever the reason, go for the low-maintenance, easy-win meal on those nights or give yourself permission to take the night off.

SCHEDULE A NIGHT OFF

Burnout is real. Planning a night off from cooking can help, and it can take many forms. Maybe you eat leftovers, order a pizza, or try a new restaurant. Maybe the primary cook hands duties to a partner, roommate, or capable child. Knowing that you have Friday night off can make preparing Thursday's dinner feel easier.

Storage Guide

Store each kind of produce in its ideal environment for maximum flavor and usability. The closer you buy to the source, the longer it will last. Veggies from your garden or the farmers' market likely will last longer than their grocery-store counterparts.

ROOM TEMPERATURE

TOMATOES
- stem removed, stem-side down, on a plate
- 1–2 days or as soon as they're ripe

SWEET POTATOES
- unwashed, in a ventilated basket or paper bag
- 2–3 weeks

REFRIGERATOR

Middle Fridge Shelf

CORN
- unhusked, in an airtight bag
- 2 days

ASPARAGUS
- ends trimmed and placed in a jar of water, covered with a loose bag
- 3 days

GREEN BEANS
- dried well, in a ventilated container
- 5–7 days

CARROTS
- unpeeled, in an airtight bag
- 2–3 weeks

Crisper Drawer

BRUSSELS SPROUTS
- whole, dried well, in an airtight container
- 3–4 days

BROCCOLI
- florets or whole, dried well, in a ventilated container
- 3–5 days

CAULIFLOWER
- florets or whole, dried well, in a ventilated container
- 3–5 days

CUCUMBERS
- whole, wrapped in dry paper towels, in a ventilated container
- 4–6 days

BELL PEPPERS
- whole, dried well, in a ventilated container
- 4–6 days

ZUCCHINI
- whole, dried well, in a ventilated container
- 5–7 days

SPINACH
- surrounded by dry paper towels, in an airtight container
- 4–7 days

KALE
- surrounded by dry paper towels, in an airtight container
- 6–8 days

Plant Proteins

A Guide to Plant Proteins

In recent years, a lot of nutrition advice has focused on protein, specifically whether you're getting enough. Omnivores often think of meat first, but many plants provide great sources of protein. And conveniently, lots of them can be stored in the pantry and are extremely easy on the budget. If you have some of these plant-based proteins on hand, you need just a vegetable and some seasoning to make a complete and satisfying meal.

To make more substantial dishes from these kitchen staples, check out the recipes that follow the lists. You'll see these veggie proteins referenced throughout this book as ways to make any recipe vegetarian.

GRAINS AND SEEDS

Chia seeds

Farro

Flaxseeds

Millet

Oats (oat milk)

Pasta, high-protein varieties
   made from lentils or chickpeas
   or whole wheat

Pumpkin seeds (pepitas)

Quinoa

Sesame seeds (tahini)

Sunflower seeds

NUTS

Almonds

Cashews

Hazelnuts

Pecans

Pine nuts (pignoli)

Pistachios

Walnuts

Nut butters

LEGUMES

Black beans

Cannellini and other white beans

Chickpeas

Kidney beans

Lentils

Peanuts

Pinto beans

Soy (edamame/soybeans,
   soy milk, tofu)

Split peas

PAN-FRIED TOFU
→ 4 to 6 servings
→ 10 grams protein per serving

ROASTED CHICKPEAS
→ 4 servings
→ 9 grams protein per ¾ cup

MISO CASHEW CREAM
→ 4 servings
→ 9 grams protein per ½ cup

HOT HONEY GRANOLA
→ 4 servings
→ 7 grams protein per 1 cup

RED LENTIL BITES
→ 4 servings
→ 13 grams protein per 6 balls

Pan-Fried Tofu

No marinating or pressing required for these easy, breezy tofu strips cooked on the stove. They're crisp around the edges and tender in the center. When I make them with firm tofu, my daughter says they have the "texture of marshmallows," which is the highest praise a nine-year-old can give a home cook.

SERVES 4 TO 6   PREP: 10 MINUTES   COOK: 15 MINUTES   TOTAL: 25 MINUTES
cutting board · knife · paper towels or dish towel · large nonstick pan · hard spatula or tongs

one 14-ounce block tofu, firm or extra-firm

1½ tablespoons cooking oil

1½ tablespoons low-sodium soy sauce or tamari

1. Drain the tofu and slice it into four equal rectangles. With paper towels or a clean dish towel, pat the rectangles dry, then slice each into batons 1 inch long.

2. In your largest nonstick pan, swirl the cooking oil to coat the bottom. To the cool pan, add the tofu batons in a single layer.

3. Place the pan over medium heat and cook until the batons turn golden brown on the bottom, 5 to 7 minutes.

4. With a hard spatula or heatproof tongs, flip the batons and cook until the other sides turn golden brown, 4 to 5 more minutes.

5. Remove the pan from the heat and pour the soy sauce evenly over the cooked tofu.

6. Return the pan to the heat and continue cooking, turning the batons often, until the tofu turns golden brown on all sides and the pan is dry, 3 to 5 more minutes.

7. Transfer the tofu to a paper towel–lined plate to cool. Serve warm or at room temperature.

NOTE: Pan-fried tofu will keep in the fridge for up to 3 days, but it will soften as it sits.

Roasted Chickpeas

These little crunchers make an irresistible snack, so this recipe makes enough for snacking *and* dinner.

MAKES 3 CUPS PREP: 10 MINUTES COOK: 20 MINUTES TOTAL: 30 MINUTES
paper towels or dish towel • large mixing bowl • rimmed baking sheet

two 15½-ounce cans chickpeas

2 tablespoons olive oil

2 teaspoons smoked paprika

1 teaspoon mild curry powder

½ teaspoon garlic powder

½ teaspoon kosher salt

black pepper

1. Preheat the oven to 425°F.

2. Drain and rinse the chickpeas. Rub them gently in paper towels or a clean dish towel to dry. Discard any skins that fall off in the process.

3. In a large mixing bowl, combine the chickpeas, olive oil, paprika, curry powder, garlic powder, salt, and a few twists of black pepper. Toss to coat evenly.

4. On an unlined rimmed baking sheet, spread out the seasoned chickpeas. Bake until the chickpeas turn golden brown and split in places, 20 to 25 minutes. Shake the pan twice during cooking.

5. On the baking sheet, let the chickpeas cool completely before transferring them to a sealable container.

NOTE: Store the chickpeas at room temperature and use them within 2 days.

VARIATIONS

Any combination of spices will work well here. Try everything bagel seasoning, a store-bought BBQ spice mix, or Dry Rub (page 240). Mix it up and use your favorites.

Miso Cashew Cream

Use this creamy, dreamy, protein-packed sauce for drizzling over *everything*. Try it in place of sour cream, for a salad dressing, or on roasted veggies, raw veggies, or noodles.

MAKES 2 CUPS   PREP: 15 MINUTES   COOK: 15 MINUTES   TOTAL: 30 MINUTES
medium mixing bowl • blender or food processor

1½ cups raw, unsalted cashews

¾ cup water, plus more for soaking and refrigerating

2 tablespoons white (shiro) miso

1 tablespoon white wine vinegar

¼ teaspoon kosher salt

1. In a medium mixing bowl, cover the cashews with boiling water and let them soak for 15 minutes.

2. Drain the soaked cashews.

3. In a blender or food processor, combine the soaked cashews, ¾ cup water, miso, vinegar, and salt. Blend until smooth.

4. Serve or let cool to room temperature and refrigerate.

NOTES: Truly raw cashews aren't safe to eat, but most store-bought packages labeled "raw" contain nuts steamed to render them safe. Soaking the cashews ensures that they're safe to eat no matter what happened before they reached your kitchen. Soaking also softens them so they blend nicely into a rich, creamy sauce.

In an airtight container, the sauce will keep in the fridge for 1 week.

 TIP The sauce will thicken in the fridge. If you're not going to use it right away, add ¼ cup more water and blend again until smooth.

VARIATIONS

Instead of boiling water, you can cover the nuts with cool water and soak them for 4 hours.

Raw cashews will result in the brightest, freshest-tasting sauce, but you can use roasted, unsalted cashews instead. Those will result in an off-white sauce with a toasty flavor.

Hot Honey Granola

This crunchy topping that you never knew you needed has the same nutrition-packed ingredients as its sweeter sibling that often goes on yogurt. The addition of Worcestershire sauce and sriracha help this granola to lean savory over sweet, so it adds great crunch to grain bowls, roasted vegetables, salads, soups, and more. It's still great on yogurt, too!

MAKES 4 CUPS   PREP: 15 MINUTES   COOK: 25 MINUTES   TOTAL: 40 MINUTES
rimmed baking sheet • parchment paper • cutting board • knife • large mixing bowl • hard spatula

---

¼ cup cooking oil

3 tablespoons honey, maple syrup, or agave syrup

2 teaspoons Worcestershire sauce

1 teaspoon sriracha or hot sauce of choice or ½ teaspoon red pepper flakes

½ teaspoon kosher salt

1½ cups rolled old-fashioned oats

½ cup roasted unsalted sunflower seeds

½ cup slivered almonds

2 tablespoons white sesame seeds

1. Preheat the oven to 300°F and line a rimmed baking sheet with parchment paper.

2. In a large mixing bowl, whisk the cooking oil, honey, Worcestershire sauce, sriracha, and salt.

3. Stir in the oats, sunflower seeds, almonds, and sesame seeds.

4. On the prepared baking sheet, spread the granola evenly in a thin layer, about ¼-inch thick. Use the flat side of a measuring cup to ensure it is an even layer and to help everything begin to stick together.

5. Bake without stirring, until golden brown and toasty, 25 to 35 minutes.

6. On the baking sheet, let the granola cool to room temperature. Once cool, break it apart into pieces.

NOTE: In an airtight container, store the granola at room temperature for up to 1 week or freeze it for up to 4 months.

Red Lentil Bites

Perfect for snacking or dipping, these crispy yet tender no-meat balls can sub for meatballs in any recipe. Make a batch and add them to sandwiches, salads, or wraps or serve them with your favorite dipping sauce, such as the honey mustard mayo from Roast Chicken and Broccoli (page 38) or Miso Cashew Cream (page 9).

MAKES 30 BALLS PREP: 35 MINUTES COOK: 15 MINUTES TOTAL: 50 MINUTES
medium mixing bowl • nonstick pan • food processor • rimmed baking sheet • parchment paper

---

1 cup raw red lentils

2 tablespoons olive oil

2 cups raw riced cauliflower

1 clove garlic

3 tablespoons tomato paste

1 teaspoon ground cumin

1 teaspoon paprika

¾ teaspoon kosher salt

VARIATION

Instead of boiling water, you can cover the beans with cool water and soak them for 4 hours.

1. In a medium mixing bowl, cover the lentils with boiling water and soak them for 15 minutes.

2. Preheat the oven to 425°F.

3. In a nonstick pan over medium heat, heat 1 tablespoon of the olive oil. Add the riced cauliflower and cook, stirring often, until tender, about 5 minutes. Transfer the cooked cauliflower to a food processor.

4. Add the garlic, tomato paste, cumin, paprika, and salt to the food processor.

5. When the lentils have finished soaking, drain them and add them to the food processor. Pulse the mixture, scraping down the sides often, until nearly all the lentils have broken apart but the mixture still looks sandy. If you squeeze a small amount together, it just barely should hold together.

6. Line a rimmed baking sheet with parchment paper and lightly oil your hands.

7. Scoop the lentil mixture in 1-tablespoon portions, roll them into balls, and place the bites on the prepared baking sheet, leaving about 2 inches of space among them.

8. Brush the tops of the lentil balls with the remaining 1 tablespoon of olive oil.

9. Bake until the balls turn golden on the outside but still feel tender in the center, 15 to 18 minutes.

10. Serve warm or let them cool on the baking sheet.

NOTES: In an airtight container, refrigerate the bites for up to 3 days. They'll soften in the fridge, but you can reheat leftovers in the microwave for 2 to 4 minutes and use them whole or crumbled.

Carrots

ROASTED CARROT AND ORZO SALAD
WITH MAPLE TAHINI DRESSING   15

CARROT QUINOA STEW WITH
GINGER AND COCONUT   18

CITRUS, CARROT, AND CHICKPEA COUSCOUS   21

ROASTED CARROTS AND WALNUTS
WITH ARUGULA CHIMICHURRI   22

BANH MI BOWLS WITH
QUICK-PICKLED CARROTS   25

CURRIED CARROT RISOTTO
WITH CRISPY SHIITAKES   27

Roasted Carrot and Orzo Salad

WITH MAPLE TAHINI DRESSING

Pasta salad meets green salad in a colorful dish for any time of year. Easily make it ahead or toss everything together just before serving. Either way, you'll taste the Maple Tahini Dressing (page 241) in every bite.

SERVES 4 TO 6   PREP: 10 MINUTES   COOK: 25 MINUTES   TOTAL: 35 MINUTES

vegetable peeler • cutting board • knife • large mixing bowl • rimmed baking sheet • parchment paper • saucepan • colander • jar or small bowl • large salad bowl

1 pound carrots

½ cup plus 1 tablespoon olive oil

1 teaspoon paprika

1 teaspoon kosher salt, plus more for the pasta

1 cup dry orzo pasta

1 batch Maple Tahini Dressing (page 241)

¾ cup shelled pistachios

5 ounces (5 cups) mixed salad greens

4 ounces feta cheese

1. Preheat the oven to 400°F.

2. Peel the carrots and slice them diagonally into 1-inch ovals.

3. In a large mixing bowl, combine the carrots with 1 tablespoon of the olive oil, paprika, and ½ teaspoon salt, coating evenly.

4. Line a rimmed baking sheet with parchment paper. Spread the carrots on it in an even layer. Bake until the carrots are tender, 20 to 25 minutes. Stir halfway through cooking.

5. Meanwhile, fill a large saucepan with water and place it over high heat. Add a generous amount of salt, up to 1 tablespoon, and bring it to a boil. When the water is boiling, add the orzo and cook according to package directions. Drain and rinse with cool water to cool the orzo before combining it with the remaining salad ingredients.

6. Let the carrots cool enough to handle, 5 to 10 minutes. It's OK if they're slightly warm, but you don't want them to wilt the greens.

CONTINUES →

7. In a large salad bowl, combine the mixed greens and orzo. Drizzle with half of the Maple Tahini Dressing. Top with the carrots and pistachios. Crumble the feta cheese over the top. Serve with the remaining dressing on the side and add more at the table as desired.

NOTE: You can roast the carrots, make the dressing, and cook the pasta up to 3 days ahead. Let everything come to room temperature and assemble to serve.

DOUBLE UP!

Make a double batch of Maple Tahini Dressing (page 241) used in this recipe and use it in Pita Crunch Salad with Roasted Brussels Sprouts (page 200).

Carrot Quinoa Stew

WITH GINGER AND COCONUT

Move over, chicken noodle. Eat this soup to get cozy on chilly evenings or when you (might) have caught a cold. A rich broth packs this soup with nutrients and can't-resist flavors. You can use rice or quinoa in the stew, mostly for texture. I love using ¼ cup of each. The rice turns tender and adds starchy thickness while the quinoa holds its chewy, springy texture.

SERVES 4   PREP: 15 MINUTES   COOK: 25 MINUTES   TOTAL: 40 MINUTES
vegetable peeler • cutting board • knife • stockpot or Dutch oven

---

12 ounces carrots

2 cloves garlic

2-inch piece fresh ginger, peeled

5 ounces baby spinach (4 cups) or 1 bunch curly kale

two 15½-ounce cans coconut milk

1 teaspoon ground turmeric

¾ teaspoon kosher salt, more if needed

2 cups low-sodium vegetable stock

½ cup uncooked quinoa, or uncooked long-grain white rice, or a combination

one 15½-ounce can cannellini beans

black pepper

plain yogurt for serving

pita or naan for serving (optional)

1. Peel the carrots and slice them into ¼-inch discs or half-moons if the carrots are thick. Peel and mince the garlic and ginger. If using baby spinach and the leaves are large, roughly chop them. If using kale, remove and discard the stems. Finely chop the leaves.

2. Open one can of coconut milk. It should have a layer of thick coconut cream on top. Scoop 2 tablespoons of it into a stockpot or Dutch oven.

3. Place the stockpot over medium heat and melt the coconut cream. Add the garlic, ginger, turmeric, and salt. Cook, stirring, until fragrant, about 2 minutes. Add the carrots and stir to coat them in the spices.

4. Add the remaining coconut milk and cream from both cans and vegetable stock and scrape any browned bits from the bottom of the stockpot.

5. Bring the stew to a simmer and add the quinoa and/or rice. If using kale, add it now. Simmer until the quinoa and carrots become tender, about 20 minutes. Adjust the heat as needed so that the stew continues to bubble gently.

6. Meanwhile, drain and rinse the beans. When the quinoa is tender, stir in the beans. If using spinach, add it now and simmer until the spinach wilts, about 5 more minutes.

7. Taste the stew and add salt if needed. The sodium in the stock and canned beans varies, so don't skip this step.

8. Divide the stew among serving bowls. Top each serving with a couple of twists of black pepper and a spoonful of yogurt. Serve with warm pita or naan if desired.

NOTE: Don't use light coconut milk for this recipe. You need the full-fat kind for the best flavor.

 Refrigerating the coconut milk before using it will help it to separate and encourage the cream to rise to the top.

Citrus, Carrot, and Chickpea Couscous

Sweet carrots and tart cranberries complement each other in every bite of this tangy couscous. It makes a light meal on its own but becomes a showstopper when spread on a platter and topped with braised meat, roasted cauliflower steaks, or seared tofu. If you want to add a little creaminess, serve the couscous with a spoonful of plain yogurt or a drizzle of Miso Cashew Cream (page 9).

SERVES 4 TO 6   PREP: 15 MINUTES   COOK: 30 MINUTES   TOTAL: 45 MINUTES

vegetable peeler • cutting board • knife • large mixing bowl • rimmed baking sheet • parchment paper • medium saucepan

---

1 pound carrots

one 15½-ounce can chickpeas

3 tablespoons olive oil

1½ teaspoons ground cumin

½ teaspoon ground ginger

½ teaspoon dried thyme

¾ teaspoon kosher salt, plus more for boiling

½ cup orange juice

1 cup water

1 cup dry regular or whole wheat couscous

⅓ cup sliced almonds

1 lemon

½ cup dried cranberries

chopped fresh parsley for garnish

1. Preheat the oven to 425°F.

2. Peel the carrots and slice them diagonally into 1-inch ovals. Drain and rinse the chickpeas.

3. In a large mixing bowl, combine the carrots and chickpeas with 1 tablespoon of the olive oil, cumin, ginger, dried thyme, and ½ teaspoon of the salt, coating evenly.

4. Line a rimmed baking sheet with parchment paper. Spread the seasoned veggies and chickpeas on it in an even layer.

5. Bake until the carrots become tender, 25 to 30 minutes. Stir halfway through cooking.

6. Meanwhile, in a medium saucepan over high heat, combine the orange juice, water, and ½ teaspoon of salt. When the mixture begins to boil, remove it from the heat, stir in the couscous, cover, and let stand for 5 minutes.

7. When the carrots become tender, sprinkle the almonds on them and continue baking until the almonds lightly toast, 4 to 5 more minutes.

8. Juice the lemon for 1 tablespoon fresh juice.

9. In the same mixing bowl used to season the veggies, whisk together the lemon juice, 2 tablespoons of olive oil, and the cranberries.

10. Fluff the couscous with a fork and add it to the carrots, chickpeas, and almonds. Stir well to combine.

11. Serve warm or refrigerate for 30 minutes and serve chilled. Just before serving, stir in the parsley.

Roasted Carrots and Walnuts
WITH ARUGULA CHIMICHURRI

The peppery arugula in this dish offers a fresh take on chimichurri sauce that doesn't rely on seasonal herbs. Use rainbow carrots to add even more color to this side dish.

SERVES 4 TO 6 PREP: 20 MINUTES COOK: 25 MINUTES TOTAL: 45 MINUTES
vegetable peeler • cutting board • knife • rimmed baking sheet • parchment paper

---

1 pound carrots

1 shallot

1 Jalapeño pepper

2 cloves garlic

1 cup walnut halves or ¾ cup walnut pieces

½ cup plus 1 tablespoon olive oil

1 teaspoon kosher salt

¼ cup red wine vinegar

3 ounces baby arugula (3 packed cups)

2 teaspoons honey

VARIATION

To make it a main dish, create a hummus bowl by serving the carrots, walnuts, and arugula chimichurri over a generous helping of hummus with warm pita on the side.

1. Preheat the oven to 425°F.

2. Peel the carrots and slice them in half lengthwise. Roughly chop the shallot and Jalapeño pepper. Peel the garlic. If using walnut halves, roughly chop them, as well.

3. Line a rimmed baking sheet with parchment paper and spread the carrots on it in an even layer. Drizzle 1 tablespoon of the olive oil on them and sprinkle with ½ teaspoon of the salt. Gently roll the carrots around to coat them evenly.

4. Roast the carrots, without stirring, until the thickest spot becomes nearly tender, 20 to 30 minutes.

5. Meanwhile, in a food processor, combine the remaining ½ cup of olive oil, vinegar, arugula, shallot, Jalapeño pepper, garlic, honey, and remaining ½ teaspoon of salt. Pulse to combine, with small flakes of arugula remaining.

6. When the carrots are nearly tender, scatter the walnuts on them and continue roasting to toast the walnuts lightly, 5 more minutes.

7. Transfer the carrots and walnuts to a serving platter. Spoon the arugula chimichurri over them. Serve warm or let them cool to room temperature.

 TIPS You can roast the carrots and walnuts and make the chimichurri up to 3 days ahead and refrigerate them. Store the carrots and the toasted walnuts in separate containers. Let everything come to room temperature before serving. If roasting ahead, don't use rainbow carrots because the purple ones will brown and the colors will bleed as they sit.

Banh Mi Bowls
WITH QUICK-PICKLED CARROTS

If you like banh mi, this weeknight-friendly bowl inspired by the Vietnamese sandwich is for you. Quick-pickled carrots, crisp lettuce leaves, and fresh herbs give the bowls color and crunch. Break the lettuce leaves apart and mix them with the other ingredients as you eat or use the leaves to scoop the other ingredients, like messy wraps.

SERVES 4   PREP: 20 MINUTES   COOK: 40 MINUTES   TOTAL: 1 HOUR

medium saucepan or rice cooker • vegetable peeler • large jar • small bowl or glass measuring cup • cutting board • knife • sauté pan • small bowl

---

- 1½ cups uncooked white or brown rice
- 10 ounces carrots, whole or preshredded to save time
- ½ cup apple cider vinegar
- ½ cup warm water
- 2 tablespoons honey
- ½ teaspoon kosher salt
- 1 tablespoon cooking oil
- 1 pound ground pork
- ¼ cup hoisin sauce
- 2 tablespoons low-sodium soy sauce or tamari
- 1 tablespoon fish sauce
- 1 cup plain yogurt
- 2 tablespoons mayonnaise
- 1 to 4 tablespoons sriracha
- 12 large leaves green leaf lettuce or other tender lettuce
- 1 cup loosely packed fresh herbs, such as basil, cilantro, and/or mint

1. On the stovetop or using a rice cooker, cook the rice according to package directions.

2. If the carrots are not preshredded, peel them and slice into ribbons with a vegetable peeler. Pack the shredded carrots into a large jar.

3. In a small bowl or glass measuring cup, whisk together the vinegar, ½ cup warm water, honey, and salt until the honey and salt dissolve. Pour the pickling liquid over the carrots and let them soak at room temperature until ready to use.

4. In a sauté pan over medium heat, heat the oil. Add the pork and cook, breaking it apart, until it mostly has cooked through but remains pink in some spots, 5 to 6 minutes.

5. While the pork cooks, whisk together the hoisin, soy, and fish sauces. Pour the sauce mixture over the pork and continue cooking, stirring often, until the pork has browned well and is sizzling, 6 to 8 more minutes.

6. In a small bowl, whisk together the yogurt, mayonnaise, and sriracha.

7. Divide the lettuce leaves among serving bowls, placing them at an angle so the tender tops stick out of the bowls. Fill the bowls with rice and pork.

CONTINUES →

8. Drain the pickled carrots and add them to one side of each bowl.

9. Garnish each bowl with herbs and top with sriracha yogurt sauce.

NOTE: You can refrigerate the quick-pickled carrots for up to 1 week.

 Repurpose the leftover pickling liquid by using it instead of the vinegar in any vinaigrette. Skip any added sweetener or salt because the pickling liquid already includes those elements.

DOUBLE UP!

The sauce in this recipe is similar to Gochujang Yogurt Sauce (page 240) but made with sriracha instead. The two are easily interchangeable, so make a double batch and use the sauce to make No-Roll Sushi Bowls (page 143), Green Bean and Ginger Wraps with Chicken (page 172), or Sweet Potatoes, Broccoli, and Gochujang Chicken (page 61).

Curried Carrot Risotto
WITH CRISPY SHIITAKES

This elegant dish has a few moving parts. But the risotto and the carrots that give it a golden hue cook hands-off in the oven. Serve it for your next holiday meal. It's vegan and gluten-free, so absolutely everyone can enjoy it.

SERVES 4   PREP: 30 MINUTES   COOK: 45 MINUTES   TOTAL: 1 HOUR 15 MINUTES

vegetable peeler • cutting board • knife • rimmed baking sheet • parchment paper • lidded oven-safe sauté pan or Dutch oven • large nonstick pan or well-seasoned cast-iron skillet • blender

12 ounces carrots

¼ cup cooking oil

1 teaspoon kosher salt, more if needed

2 cloves garlic

1-inch piece fresh ginger, peeled

1 small yellow or white onion

1 teaspoon mild yellow curry powder

1 cup Arborio rice

3 cups low-sodium vegetable stock

1 cup roasted unsalted cashews

12 ounces shiitake mushrooms

one 15-ounce can light coconut milk

1. In the oven, arrange a rack in the lower position and another in the upper position. Preheat it to 425°F.

2. Peel the carrots and slice them into ½-inch discs.

3. Line a rimmed baking sheet with parchment paper. Spread the carrots on it, drizzle them with 1 tablespoon of the cooking oil, and sprinkle with ¼ teaspoon of the salt. Stir to coat evenly.

4. On the upper rack of the oven, roast the carrots until tender, 20 to 25 minutes. Stir halfway through cooking.

5. Meanwhile, peel and mince the garlic and ginger and dice the onion.

6. In a large, lidded, oven-safe sauté pan or Dutch oven over medium heat, add 1 tablespoon of cooking oil and the onion and cook, stirring constantly, until the onion becomes translucent, 5 to 7 minutes.

7. Add the garlic, ginger, curry powder, and ¼ teaspoon of salt and cook until fragrant, about 2 more minutes.

8. Pour the rice over the onions and stir until the rice looks shiny and coated in spices. Pour the vegetable stock over the rice and bring it to a simmer. Increase the heat if needed to simmer quickly.

CONTINUES →

9. Cover the rice and place it on the lower rack of the pre-heated oven. Cook until the rice absorbs all the liquids and becomes tender, 18 minutes. If it's not tender after 18 minutes, cover and return it to the oven until it is, lifting the lid to check on it every 2 to 3 minutes.

10. While the rice cooks, roughly chop the cashews. Stem the mushrooms and slice the caps into $1/4$-inch slices.

11. In a large nonstick pan or well-seasoned cast-iron skillet over medium heat, add the remaining 2 tablespoons of cooking oil and the mushrooms and cook until the bottoms turn a deep golden brown.

12. Stir the mushrooms to brown on both sides. The mushrooms have finished when they've reduced to a quarter of their original size and become crispy around the edges, 8 to 10 minutes.

13. Add the cashews and $1/2$ teaspoon of salt and cook for 2 more minutes to toast the cashews lightly.

14. When the carrots have finished cooking, transfer them to a blender. Add the coconut milk and blend until smooth.

15. When the rice has finished cooking, add the carrot mixture to the risotto. Stir the risotto about 20 times to thicken it. Taste and add salt if needed.

16. Divide the risotto among the serving bowls and top each with mushrooms and cashews.

Broccoli

Broccoli Caesar-ish Salad

WITH TOASTED BREAD CRUMBS

This salad skips the anchovies and egg yolks of its classic namesake, but the dressing still has all the creamy, tangy, richness of the original. Toasted bread crumbs deliver a satisfying crunch in every bite that doesn't require chasing croutons around the plate.

SERVES 4   PREP: 25 MINUTES   COOK: 10 MINUTES   TOTAL: 35 MINUTES
cutting board · knife · large mixing bowl · medium nonstick pan · small bowl · whisk · grater

---

1 large head broccoli
  (1½ pounds or
  10 ounces florets)

2 hearts romaine lettuce

3 tablespoons unsalted butter

1 cup panko bread crumbs

¼ teaspoon kosher salt

1 lemon

¼ cup mayonnaise

¼ cup plain yogurt

2 teaspoons low-sodium soy
  sauce or tamari

2 teaspoons Dijon mustard

1 clove garlic

¾ cup freshly grated
  Parmesan cheese

black pepper

1. If using a head of broccoli, chop it into bite-size florets. Halve store-bought florets lengthwise. You should have about 2½ cups. Add them to the mixing bowl.

2. Rinse, dry, and chop the lettuce. Add it to the broccoli.

3. In a medium nonstick pan over medium heat, melt the butter. Add the bread crumbs and salt and cook, stirring often, until the panko turns golden brown, 7 to 10 minutes. Reduce the heat if the panko shows signs of burning.

4. Remove the pan from the heat and zest 1 lemon into the panko. Stir to combine.

5. Juice the lemon for 2 tablespoons of fresh juice.

6. In a small bowl, whisk together the mayonnaise, yogurt, lemon juice, soy sauce, and mustard. Grate the garlic directly into the dressing and stir to combine.

7. Gradually add the dressing to the broccoli and lettuce, tossing as you go. Dress to your liking: all of it for a heavily dressed salad or less for a lighter touch.

8. Add half of the toasted bread crumbs to the bowl and grate ½ cup of Parmesan cheese on the salad. Gently stir to mix well.

CONTINUES →

9. Grate ¼ cup more Parmesan on the salad and top with the remaining bread crumbs and black pepper to taste. Serve immediately.

NOTE: This salad tastes best as soon as you make it, before the breadcrumbs soak up the dressing and lose their crunch.

 Use any leftover dressing as a veggie dip or marinade for chicken, fish, or tofu.

VARIATIONS

To work another veggie into this dish, substitute 2 cups of baby spinach for 1 heart of romaine lettuce.

To make it a main dish, add your protein of choice, such as crispy chicken tenders, grilled chicken, or seared salmon. To make your main dish vegetarian, top it with Roasted Chickpeas (page 6).

Thai Broccoli Slaw

This easier twist on som tam has all the salty, sour, crunchy heat of the original. Made with green papaya, traditional som tam calls for using a mortar and pestle. If you have one and want to use it, go for it. Otherwise, just stir everything together in a bowl. Look for bagged broccoli slaw in your grocery store's produce section. If it includes shredded carrot and/or cabbage, even better. If you love spice, this recipe offers a great opportunity to crank it up!

SERVES 4 TO 6   PREP: 20 MINUTES   TOTAL: 20 MINUTES
cutting board • knife • jar or small bowl • large mortar and pestle (optional) • mixing bowl

---

½ cup roasted unsalted peanuts

20 cherry or grape tomatoes

1 small lime

1 clove garlic

2 tablespoons low-sodium soy sauce or tamari

1 tablespoon fish sauce

1 tablespoon honey

½ teaspoon sriracha or red pepper flakes

12 ounces broccoli slaw

½ cup fresh cilantro and/or basil

VARIATION

To make it vegetarian, substitute low-sodium soy sauce or tamari for the fish sauce, meaning 3 tablespoons total of soy sauce or tamari.

1. Roughly chop the peanuts. Halve the tomatoes lengthwise. Squeeze the lime for 1 tablespoon of fresh juice. Peel and grate the garlic.

2. In a small bowl or jar, whisk or shake together the soy sauce, fish sauce, lime juice, honey, garlic, and sriracha to make the dressing.

3. If not using a mortar and pestle, skip this step. Add roughly half of the broccoli to the mortar along with 1 teaspoon of the dressing. Gently pound the broccoli with the pestle to tenderize it. Transfer the tenderized broccoli to a large mixing bowl. Repeat the process in the mortar and pestle with the remaining broccoli and then add it to the mixing bowl.

4. Add the broccoli slaw, dressing, and tomatoes to the mixing bowl and coat evenly.

5. Top with the chopped peanuts and herbs and serve immediately or refrigerate for up to 4 hours. If chilling the dish, the dressing will run to the bottom of the bowl. Before serving, toss to coat and then top with peanuts and herbs.

 TIP This slaw tastes great with pretty much anything grilled. Try it with your favorite meat-based or vegetarian sausages.

Broccoli Piccata
WITH PARMESAN CHEESE

The capers, garlic, lemon, and shallots in tangy piccata sauce can make any vegetable taste like it has basked in the summer sun. Featuring skillet-charred broccoli, this dish will shine as the star of your dinner table.

SERVES 4   PREP: 10 MINUTES   COOK: 15 MINUTES   TOTAL: 25 MINUTES

cutting board · knife · small bowl · whisk · hard spatula · large lidded sauté pan · cheese grater

---

1 large head broccoli
  (1½ pounds)

1 shallot

1 clove garlic

2 tablespoons water

¼ teaspoon kosher salt

1 large lemon

1 tablespoon cooking oil

2 tablespoons unsalted butter

2 tablespoons capers

Parmesan cheese for serving

1. Slice off the lower portion of the broccoli stems, leaving about 3 inches intact. Place the broccoli on its side and cut into ½-inch-thick slices. Chop any extra florets that remain.

2. Dice the shallot and mince the garlic.

3. In a small bowl, whisk together the shallot, garlic, water, and ¼ teaspoon of the salt.

4. Juice the lemon for 1½ tablespoons of fresh juice.

5. In your largest lidded sauté pan over medium heat, heat the cooking oil. Add the broccoli to the heated oil and sear, without moving, until golden brown on one side, 3 to 4 minutes.

6. Use a hard spatula to flip the broccoli. Pour the shallot-garlic mixture around the broccoli and immediately cover. Cook, covered, for 2 minutes, shaking the pan gently to distribute the broccoli as it cooks.

7. Uncover and continue cooking until tender, 3 to 5 minutes more. Broccoli doneness is highly personal, so cook to your preferred texture.

8. Transfer the broccoli to a serving plate, leaving the sauté pan over medium heat. To the heated pan add the butter, scraping the pan gently to release any browned bits.

9. Remove the pan from the heat and stir in the lemon juice and capers.

10. Spoon the sauce over the broccoli, generously grate Parmesan cheese on it, and serve warm.

Roast Chicken and Broccoli
WITH HONEY MUSTARD MAYO

Sheet-pan meals = easy cleanup. This recipe calls for two sheet pans so the broccoli has enough space for the edges to crisp. It seems straightforward, but don't underestimate the power of creamy honey mustard to make an ordinary weeknight meal feel (and taste) special.

SERVES 4   PREP: 20 MINUTES   COOK: 25 MINUTES   TOTAL: 45 MINUTES
cutting board · knife · 2 rimmed baking sheets · parchment paper · small bowl

2 large heads broccoli
(3 pounds or
20 ounces florets)

2 tablespoons olive oil

1¾ teaspoons kosher salt

1½ pounds boneless, skinless
chicken thighs

black pepper

¼ cup mayonnaise

3 tablespoons smooth
Dijon mustard

3 tablespoons honey

2 tablespoons
stone-ground mustard

1 teaspoon red wine vinegar

1. In the oven, arrange a rack in the lower position and another in the upper position. Preheat it to 425°F.

2. If using a head of broccoli, chop it into florets. To use the stalk, slice off the tough outer layer, removing about ⅛ inch on each side and chopping the stalk into ½-inch slices. Halve store-bought florets lengthwise. You should have about 6 cups, which may seem like a lot, but they'll reduce in the oven.

3. On an unlined rimmed baking sheet, spread the broccoli in an even layer. Drizzle the olive oil over it and sprinkle with ¾ teaspoon of the salt. Gently mix with your hands to coat evenly.

4. Line a second rimmed baking sheet with parchment paper. Lay the chicken thighs out flat on it and season them with salt and a few twists of black pepper.

5. Place both sheet pans in the oven, broccoli on the top rack, and bake for 10 minutes.

6. Meanwhile, make the honey mustard mayo. In a small bowl, whisk together mayonnaise, Dijon mustard, honey, stone-ground mustard, and vinegar. Reserve ¼ cup as a cooking sauce for the chicken. Set aside.

CONTINUES →

7. After 10 minutes, remove the sheet pans from the oven. Generously coat the tops of the thighs with the reserved ¼ cup of honey mustard mayo. Gently stir the broccoli so it cooks evenly.

8. Return both pans to the oven, this time with the chicken on the top rack. Continue cooking until the chicken reaches 165°F in the thickest part and the broccoli becomes tender, 10 to 15 more minutes.

9. Plate and serve warm with extra honey mustard mayo on the side.

VARIATION

To make it vegetarian, use Red Lentil Bites (page 13) instead of chicken. They'll finish cooking in 15 to 18 minutes total, ahead of the broccoli. Skip brushing them with honey mustard mayo and serve the sauce on the side for dipping.

 TIP I like to use two types of mustard in this sauce—a combination of creamy Dijon and stone-ground mustards give the sauce a balanced texture. But if you just have one type of mustard in your fridge, use that one for the full amount of mustard—no need to go out and purchase a second type.

Salerno Spaghetti
WITH BROCCOLINI

The lacy edges of fried eggs paired with garlicky oil and toasted bread crumbs create a meal truly greater than the sum of its parts. This is my desert-island dish. It's also a great way to use parsley languishing in the fridge. The large nonstick pan cooks three components, so give yourself time to coordinate the moving parts.

SERVES 4   PREP: 15 MINUTES   COOK: 40 MINUTES   TOTAL: 55 MINUTES
stockpot · cutting board · knife · large nonstick pan · small bowls · large mixing bowl

¼ teaspoon kosher salt, plus more for the pasta and eggs

2 bunches broccolini (12 ounces)

½ cup fresh flat or curly parsley

2 cloves garlic

¼ cup olive oil

½ teaspoon red pepper flakes

3 tablespoons unsalted butter

1 cup panko bread crumbs

zest from 1 lemon

1 pound dry spaghetti

1¼ cups freshly grated Parmesan cheese

4 large eggs

black pepper

1. Fill a stockpot half full with water, place it over medium-high heat, and salt it generously, about 1 tablespoon. Don't worry about measuring but also don't skimp. Bring the water to a boil.

2. While you wait for the water to boil, stem the broccolini and discard the stems. If any stalks are noticeably thicker than the others, halve them lengthwise. Mince the parsley and garlic.

3. In a large nonstick pan over medium heat, heat 2 table-spoons of the olive oil. When the oil shimmers, add the garlic and red pepper flakes and cook, stirring constantly, until fragrant but not browned, 1 to 2 minutes. Don't step away from the pan. The garlic can burn quickly. Drain the garlic oil into a small bowl.

4. Return the pan to medium heat and melt the butter. Add the bread crumbs and ¼ teaspoon salt and cook, stirring often, until the panko turns golden brown, 7 to 10 minutes. Reduce the heat if the panko shows signs of burning.

5. Remove the pan from the heat, zest the lemon into the panko, stir to combine, and transfer the lemon panko to a small bowl. Wipe the pan and set it aside.

6. The stockpot water should be boiling by now. Add the pasta and set a timer according to the package directions. When 4 minutes remain, add the broccolini to the pasta.

7. Reserve 1 cup of the pasta water, drain the pasta and broccolini, and transfer them to a large mixing bowl.

CONTINUES →

8. Add the garlic oil and 1 cup of the grated Parmesan cheese. Stir and toss everything as you slowly add the pasta water. The evenly coated pasta should look creamy, and you may not need all the pasta water. Cover the bowl to keep the pasta warm.

9. Place the nonstick pan over medium-high heat and add the remaining 2 tablespoons of olive oil. When the oil is hot, crack 4 eggs in it. Season them with salt and black pepper to taste. Cook until the whites nearly set, 2 to 4 minutes. Cover the pan, remove it from the heat, and let the eggs finish cooking from the residual heat.

10. Stir three-quarters of the toasted bread crumbs and all the parsley into the pasta.

11. Divide the pasta among four serving plates or bowls and top each portion with a fried egg, the reserved bread crumbs, and the remaining grated Parmesan cheese.

Broccoli, Cashew, and Chicken Meatball Skillet

You can prep this one-pan meatball skillet ahead of time, and if you do, you can cook it in less time than it takes to get an order from your favorite takeout spot.

SERVES 4   PREP: 25 MINUTES   COOK: 30 MINUTES   TOTAL: 55 MINUTES
large saucepan or rice cooker • cutting board • knife • medium mixing bowl • large sauté pan with a lid

1½ cups uncooked white or
brown rice

1 large head broccoli
(1½ pounds or
10 ounces florets)

3 green onions

1½-inch piece fresh
ginger, peeled

3 cloves garlic

1 large egg

½ cup panko bread crumbs

1 teaspoon kosher salt

½ teaspoon garlic powder

1 pound ground chicken

2 tablespoons cooking oil

½ cup low-sodium chicken
broth or stock

¼ cup low-sodium soy
sauce or tamari

¼ cup hoisin sauce

1 tablespoon honey

¼ cup water

1 tablespoon cornstarch

1 cup roasted,
unsalted cashews

white sesame seeds for garnish

VARIATION

To make it vegetarian, use
Red Lentil Bites (page 13)
or 16 ounces of cubed
extra-firm tofu. Stir in the
chopped green onions
with the cashews.

1. On the stovetop or using a rice cooker, cook the rice according to package directions.

2. If using a head of broccoli, chop it into florets. Halve store-bought florets lengthwise. You should have about 3 cups. Finely chop the green onions. Mince the ginger and garlic.

3. In a medium bowl, whisk together the egg, bread crumbs, salt, garlic powder, and green onions until smooth.

4. Add the ground chicken and mix to combine evenly.

5. Spoon out approximately 1½ tablespoons of the meatball mixture and, with wet hands, roll it into a ball. Repeat with the remaining mixture to form about 20 meatballs.

6. In a large sauté pan over medium heat, heat the oil and, in a single layer, cook the meatballs until well browned on one side, 3 to 4 minutes.

7. With heatproof tongs, gently flip the meatballs and continue cooking for 3 to 4 more minutes.

8. Meanwhile, make the sauce. In a small bowl, whisk together the broth, soy sauce, hoisin sauce, honey, and garlic. Pour the sauce over the meatballs.

9. In the same bowl, whisk together ¼ cup water and the cornstarch and pour it over the meatballs, gently stirring it into the sauce and releasing the meatballs from the pan.

10. Scatter the broccoli florets over the meatballs, cover, reduce the heat to medium-low, and simmer until the meatballs cook through and the broccoli becomes tender, 4 to 6 more minutes.

11. Uncover and gently stir in the cashews. Serve warm over rice if desired.

 TIP You can assemble the meatballs and refrigerate them for up to 24 hours or cook them and store in the freezer for up to 4 months.

Broccoli and Cheese Everything Bagel Strata

The next time you grab bagels for breakfast, order two extra everything bagels and use them to make this savory egg casserole. If you have any leftover strata slices to enjoy the next day, sear them in a buttered pan like French toast.

SERVES 4   PREP: 15 MINUTES   COOK: 1 HOUR 15 MINUTES   TOTAL: 1 HOUR 30 MINUTES

cutting board · knife · large lidded sauté pan · medium mixing bowl · 9-by-5-inch loaf pan · rimmed baking sheet

1 large head broccoli (1½ pounds or 10 ounces florets)

¼ cup water

½ teaspoon kosher salt

2 everything bagels

6 large eggs

black pepper

1¼ cups milk

¼ cup heavy cream

nonstick cooking spray

6 ounces (1½ cups) shredded Cheddar cheese

2 teaspoons everything bagel seasoning (optional)

1. If using a head of broccoli, chop it into florets. Halve store-bought florets lengthwise. You should have about 3 cups.

2. In your largest lidded sauté pan over medium-high heat, combine the water and ¼ teaspoon of the salt. Add the broccoli in a single layer. As soon as the water begins to simmer, cover the pan and cook for 2 minutes.

3. Uncover and continue cooking until the florets turn bright green and tender and all the water has cooked off, 4 to 6 minutes. Use a slotted spoon to transfer the broccoli to a paper towel–lined plate to drain and cool.

4. While the broccoli cools, slice the bagels into bite-size pieces.

5. In a mixing bowl, whisk together the eggs, ¼ teaspoon of salt, and a few twists of black pepper. Add the milk and cream and whisk until smooth.

6. Spray the loaf pan with nonstick cooking spray. Scatter half of the bagel pieces in the pan. Add all but a few of the broccoli florets, 1 cup of the cheese, and the remaining bagel pieces.

7. Add the egg mixture slowly and evenly. Top the strata with the remaining broccoli florets, cheese, and everything bagel seasoning if using. Let the strata rest for at least 15 minutes, while the oven heats in the next step, or overnight. See note.

CONTINUES →

8. When ready to bake, preheat the oven to 350°F with the rack in the middle position.

9. To catch any drips, place the strata on an unlined rimmed baking sheet and bake until golden brown on top and fully set in the center, 55 to 60 minutes. An instant read thermometer should register 160°F in the center.

10. Let the strata cool for 5 minutes before slicing and serving.

NOTE: You can assemble and cover the strata and refrigerate it overnight. Let it come to room temperature before baking.

Sweet Potatoes

RED LENTIL AND SWEET POTATO SOUP
WITH CUMIN   51

SWEET POTATO TORTA   52

SWEET POTATO COBB SALAD   55

SWEET POTATO POTSTICKERS   58

SWEET POTATOES, BROCCOLI,
AND GOCHUJANG CHICKEN   61

Red Lentil and Sweet Potato Soup
WITH CUMIN

Hearty veggies and warm spices join forces to create this nourishing soup. I love it as is, but my kids prefer it pureed with a can of coconut milk. Either way, it will warm you up on chilly winter evenings. It also freezes well, so keep some for leftovers, too.

SERVES 4 PREP: 10 MINUTES COOK: 30 MINUTES TOTAL: 40 MINUTES
vegetable peeler • cutting board • knife • large lidded sauté pan or Dutch oven

---

1½ pounds sweet potatoes

1 red bell pepper

2 cloves garlic

1 small red onion

1 tablespoon cooking oil

½ teaspoon kosher salt

1½ teaspoons ground cumin

1 teaspoon smoked paprika

½ teaspoon ground turmeric

⅛ teaspoon ground cinnamon

1 bay leaf

1 cup dry red lentils

one 15½-ounce can crushed tomatoes or tomato sauce

6 cups low-sodium vegetable stock

1 small lemon

plain yogurt or Miso Cashew Cream (page 9) for serving

chopped fresh parsley for garnish

pita or flatbread for serving (optional)

1. Slice the sweet potatoes, peeled first or peels on, into ½-inch cubes. Dice the bell pepper, mince the garlic, and dice the onion.

2. In a large lidded sauté pan or Dutch oven over medium heat, heat the cooking oil. Add the onion, bell pepper, and salt. Cook, stirring often, until the onion turns golden brown and very soft, 8 to 10 minutes.

3. Add the garlic, cumin, paprika, turmeric, cinnamon, bay leaf, and lentils. Stir for 2 minutes.

4. Add the crushed tomatoes, stock, and sweet potatoes and bring to a simmer. Cover and reduce the heat to medium-low. Simmer until the sweet potatoes and lentils become tender, 15 to 25 minutes.

5. Meanwhile, juice the lemon for 1 tablespoon of fresh juice.

6. Remove the soup from the heat, discard the bay leaf, and stir in the lemon juice. Taste and add salt if needed.

7. Ladle the soup into bowls, top with yogurt or Miso Cashew Cream and parsley, and serve with pita or flatbread if desired.

NOTE: As this soup sits, the lentils will continue to soak up liquid, turning into more of a stew. You can enjoy it that way or thin it with water if you like it lighter.

Sweet Potato Torta

Mexican torta with tender beans and other toppings serves as the inspiration for this meal, but don't expect to pick it up with your hands. You'll need a fork and knife.

SERVES 4   PREP: 15 MINUTES   COOK: 35 MINUTES   TOTAL: 50 MINUTES
rimmed baking sheet • parchment paper • cutting board • knife • small saucepan • large nonstick pan

---

1½ pounds sweet potatoes

1 tablespoon olive oil

½ teaspoon kosher salt, plus more for the eggs

1 clove garlic

1 small yellow, white, or red onion

2 tablespoons cooking oil

1 teaspoon ground cumin

one 15-ounce can black beans

4 large eggs

1 large avocado

black pepper

fresh cilantro for serving

salsa or pico de gallo for serving

1. Preheat the oven to 400°F and line a rimmed baking sheet with parchment paper.

2. Cut the sweet potatoes, peels on, lengthwise into ½-inch-thick slices. Add them in a single layer to the prepared baking sheet, grouped into four large "toasts" with a few smaller slices on the side.

3. Drizzle the sweet potato slices with the olive oil and sprinkle with the salt. Flip them to coat both sides.

4. Bake the sweet potatoes, without turning, until a fork easily pierces them but they still hold their shape, 20 to 25 minutes.

5. Meanwhile, mince the garlic and dice the onion. Reserve ¼ cup of diced onions for serving.

6. In a small saucepan over medium heat, heat 1 tablespoon of the cooking oil. Add the remaining onions and cook until translucent, 5 to 6 minutes.

7. Add the garlic and cumin and stir until fragrant, about 2 more minutes.

8. Add the beans, including the liquid from the can, and simmer for 5 to 7 minutes. While simmering, gently mash the beans with a spatula or spoon.

9. Remove the pan from the heat and cover it to keep the beans warm.

CONTINUES →

10. When the potatoes almost have finished baking, place your biggest nonstick pan over medium-high heat and heat 1 tablespoon of cooking oil. Crack the eggs in the oil. Cook until the whites nearly set. Cover the pan, remove it from the heat, and let the eggs finish cooking from the residual heat.

11. Peel, pit, and slice the avocado.

12. Plate the sweet potato tortas. Spoon the black beans over the potatoes and top each serving with a fried egg. Season with salt and black pepper to taste.

13. Serve with the reserved onions, avocado, cilantro, and salsa.

Sweet Potato Cobb Salad

Roasted sweet potatoes add a caramelized sweetness to a medley of fresh ingredients. They also give this otherwise classic cobb salad a fall vibe, but you can enjoy it any time of year.

SERVES 4　PREP: 15 MINUTES　COOK: 35 MINUTES　TOTAL: 50 MINUTES

small bowl · 16-ounce jar with a lid · cutting board · knife · 2 rimmed baking sheets · parchment paper · medium saucepan with a lid · medium mixing bowl · small bowl or jar · hard spatula

1½ pounds sweet potatoes

1 tablespoon olive oil

½ teaspoon kosher salt

10 strips uncooked bacon

2 hearts romaine lettuce or 8 ounces mixed greens

4 large eggs

1 large avocado

1 batch Balsamic Vinaigrette (page 242)

4 ounces blue, Gorgonzola, or feta cheese

1 batch Pickled Red Onions (page 245)

black pepper

1. In the oven, arrange a rack in the lower position and another in the upper position. Preheat it to 400°F.

2. Cut the sweet potatoes, peels on, down the narrow side into ½-inch-thick rounds. Line a rimmed baking sheet with parchment paper. Add the potatoes in a single layer to the prepared baking sheet. Drizzle the potatoes with the olive oil and sprinkle with ½ teaspoon of kosher salt.

3. Bake the sweet potatoes on the upper rack, without turning, until a fork easily pierces them but they still hold their shape, 20 to 25 minutes.

4. Line a second baking sheet with parchment paper and spread the bacon on it in a single layer. Cook the bacon on the lower rack until golden brown and crisp, 15 to 20 minutes.

5. Meanwhile, boil the eggs. In a medium lidded saucepan over high heat, add the eggs and enough water to cover them by 1 inch. Bring the water to a boil. As soon as the water is boiling, remove the pan from the heat and cover it. Let the eggs rest, covered, for 10 minutes.

6. While the eggs rest, chop the lettuce.

7. Fill a medium mixing bowl with water and ice. After the eggs have been resting for 10 minutes, use a slotted spoon to transfer the eggs to the ice water for 2 to 3 minutes. The ice water will loosen the peels, making them easier to remove, and prevent the yolks from overcooking.

CONTINUES →

8. The sweet potatoes and bacon should have finished cooking by now. Transfer the bacon to a paper towel–lined plate to cool.

9. Peel and chop the eggs. Peel, pit, and slice the avocado.

10. Assemble the salad by spreading the lettuce on a large serving platter or bowl or dividing it among serving plates. Drizzle the lettuce with half of the Balsamic Vinaigrette. Add the sweet potatoes, eggs, and avocados. Crumble the bacon, cheese, and Pickled Red Onions on the salad and finish with a few twists of black pepper and more Balsamic Vinaigrette to taste.

NOTE: You can prep everything except the avocado up to 3 days ahead, but peel the eggs just before serving.

DOUBLE UP!

Make a double batch of Balsamic Vinaigrette (page 242) in this recipe and use it to make Farro Caprese (page 150).

 TIP This recipe uses Pickled Red Onions (page 245), but you may not need all of them for the salad. If you have any left over, use them to make Green Goddess Grain Bowls with Asparagus and Chicken (page 183).

Sweet Potato Potstickers

The tender filling contrasts nicely with the crisp wrappers and the salty sauce. If you've never made potstickers before, you're in for a treat. Put on a podcast or your favorite tunes and give yourself a little extra time to fill and shape them. Double the fun by recruiting a helper to lend a hand.

MAKES 24 POTSTICKERS   PREP: 40 MINUTES   COOK: 10 MINUTES   TOTAL: 50 MINUTES
vegetable peeler • box grater • medium mixing bowl • small bowl or jar • parchment paper • baking sheet • large nonstick pan with a lid

---

12 ounces sweet potatoes

1½-inch piece fresh ginger, peeled

¼ bunch fresh chives, plus more for garnish

½ teaspoon kosher salt

¼ cup low-sodium soy sauce or tamari

1 tablespoon rice vinegar

1 teaspoon chili garlic sauce

24 square or round potsticker or dumpling wrappers

1 tablespoon cooking oil, more if needed

¼ cup water

1. Peel the sweet potatoes and grate them through the largest holes on a box grater into a medium mixing bowl.

2. Mince or grate the ginger and finely chop the chives. Add the ginger, chives, and salt to the potatoes. Stir to combine.

3. To make the dipping sauce, combine the soy sauce, vinegar, and chili garlic sauce in a small bowl or jar.

4. Line a baking sheet with parchment paper, fill a small bowl with water, and dampen a paper towel.

5. Fill 1 dumpling or potsticker wrapper with 1 tablespoon of the potato mixture. Dip your fingers in the bowl of water and run them around the edges of each wrapper. Join the edges and pinch them closed tightly, pressing out any air.

6. Place the finished potstickers on the prepared baking sheet and cover with the damp paper towel.

7. When you've made all the potstickers, place your largest lidded nonstick pan over medium heat and add the cooking oil. When the oil shimmers, add the potstickers in a single layer and cook without moving them until the bottoms turn golden brown, about 3 minutes. If your pan isn't large enough to cook all the potstickers at once, work in batches, adding more oil if the pan dries out between batches.

8. Pour ¼ cup water down the side of the pan and cover. Cook for 5 minutes. To test for doneness, remove 1 potsticker and slice it open to see if the filling has cooked.

9. Remove the lid and continue cooking, uncovered, until all the water evaporates.

10. Serve the potstickers with extra chives on top and the dipping sauce on the side.

Sweet Potatoes, Broccoli, and Gochujang Chicken

If you like spicy-sweet, you're going to love this multilayered dish. The natural sweetness of the sweet potato creates a creamy base for savory broccoli and sweet-spicy gochujang glaze. For the glaze, buy gochujang *sauce*, which has a balanced combination of flavors compared to much spicier gochujang paste.

SERVES 4   PREP: 20 MINUTES   COOK: 30 MINUTES   TOTAL: 50 MINUTES
cutting board · knife · 2 rimmed baking sheets · parchment paper · small bowl

---

four 10-ounce sweet potatoes

1 large head broccoli
(1½ pounds or
10 ounces florets)

4 stalks green onions

2 tablespoons cooking oil

1¼ teaspoons kosher salt

1½ pounds boneless, skinless
chicken thighs

black pepper

3 tablespoons honey

2 tablespoons gochujang sauce

1 teaspoon rice vinegar

1 batch Gochujang Yogurt
Sauce (page 240)

1. In the oven, arrange a rack in the lower position and another in the upper position. Preheat it to 400°F.

2. Halve the sweet potatoes, peels on, lengthwise. If using a head of broccoli, chop it into florets. To use the stalk, slice off the tough outer layer, removing about ⅛ inch on each side and chopping the stalk into ½-inch slices. Halve store-bought florets lengthwise. You should have about 3 cups.

3. Thinly slice the green onions.

4. Line two rimmed baking sheets with parchment paper. On the first, line up the sweet potatoes, cut sides up. Scatter the broccoli around the sweet potatoes. Drizzle the oil over the vegetables and sprinkle them with ¾ teaspoon of the salt. Toss the broccoli gently to coat evenly. Flip the seasoned sweet potatoes, cut sides down.

5. On the second prepared baking sheet, lay out the chicken thighs and season the tops with ½ teaspoon of the salt and a few twists of the black pepper.

6. In a small bowl, whisk together the honey, 2 tablespoons of the gochujang sauce, and the rice vinegar to create a glaze. Brush the glaze generously over the tops and sides of the chicken, letting any extra drip onto the parchment.

CONTINUES →

7. Bake the chicken on the upper rack of the oven and the veggies on the lower rack for 20 to 25 minutes. Gently stir the broccoli halfway through cooking. When done, the thickest part of the chicken should measure 165°F, and a fork should pierce the broccoli and sweet potatoes easily.

8. When the chicken and veggies have finished cooking, remove both sheets from the oven, but leave it on. Roughly chop the chicken on a cutting board, then return it to the baking sheet and stir it to combine with any remaining glaze on the baking sheet.

9. Divide the sweet potatoes, cut sides up, among four serving plates. With a masher or hard spatula, gently flatten the sweet potatoes.

10. Top the sweet potatoes with broccoli, chicken, and green onions. Drizzle the Gochujang Yogurt Sauce over everything and serve.

DOUBLE UP!

The sauce in this recipe is similar to Gochujang Yogurt Sauce (page 240). The two are easily interchangeable, so make a double batch and use the sauce to make No-Roll Sushi Bowls (page 143), Green Bean and Ginger Wraps with Chicken (page 172), and/or Banh Mi Bowls with Quick-Pickled Carrots (page 25).

VARIATION

To make it vegetarian, use two 15½-ounce cans of chickpeas instead of chicken. Keep an eye on them as they cook and stir them often to prevent burning. They should cook in about 15 minutes.

Cauliflower

Warm Cauliflower Salad with Pistachios

A great vegetable salad easily makes veggies the star of any meal, and this one will outshine anything served alongside it. The warm, tangy shallot vinaigrette works well on just about any vegetable, but it works best when paired with the nutty flavors of roasted cauliflower.

SERVES 4   PREP: 10 MINUTES   COOK: 20 MINUTES   TOTAL: 30 MINUTES
cutting board · knife · rimmed baking sheet · small saucepan

1 medium head cauliflower
    (2 pounds or
    12 ounces florets)

¼ cup plus 1 tablespoon
    olive oil

½ teaspoon kosher salt

2 ounces (2 cups) baby arugula

1 shallot

2 tablespoons apple
    cider vinegar

2 teaspoons Dijon mustard

1 teaspoon honey

½ cup shelled pistachios

black pepper

1. Preheat the oven to 425°F.

2. If using a head of cauliflower, chop it into florets. Halve store-bought florets lengthwise. You should have about 4 cups.

3. On an unlined rimmed baking sheet, spread the cauliflower in an even layer. Drizzle 1 tablespoon of the olive oil on it and sprinkle evenly with the salt. Stir gently to coat.

4. Roast the cauliflower until tender and golden in spots, 20 to 30 minutes, stirring halfway through cooking.

5. Meanwhile, finely chop the arugula and dice the shallot.

6. In a small saucepan over medium heat, whisk together the shallots, vinegar, mustard, and honey until just bubbling. Remove from the heat and whisk in ¼ cup of olive oil.

7. Transfer the roasted cauliflower to a serving bowl and pour half of the vinaigrette on it, stirring gently to coat.

8. Add the arugula and pistachios and stir again. Add more vinaigrette to taste or serve it on the side.

9. Finish the salad with a few twists of black pepper and serve warm.

Cauliflower Pasta Bake

You won't have to ration the crispy edges of this dish because broiling it gives every bite great crunch. If you like spice, use an arrabbiata-style marinara sauce.

SERVES 8   PREP: 20 MINUTES   COOK: 20 MINUTES   TOTAL: 40 MINUTES

stockpot • cutting board • knife • medium bowl • box grater, if grating cheeses yourself • rimmed baking sheet

---

kosher salt for the pot

1 medium head cauliflower
(2 pounds or
12 ounces florets)

1 pound uncooked pasta shells

one 24-ounce jar
marinara sauce

6 ounces shredded mozzarella
cheese (1½ cups)

½ cup freshly, finely grated
Parmesan cheese

nonstick cooking spray

3 ounces pancetta,
thinly sliced

fresh basil for garnish

VARIATION

To make it vegetarian, replace the pancetta with 6 ounces of thinly sliced or crumbled vegan sausage.

---

1. Fill a stockpot half full with water, place it over medium-high heat, and salt it generously, about 1 tablespoon. Don't worry about measuring but don't skimp. Bring the water to a boil.

2. If your oven doesn't have a dedicated broiler, use the main compartment. Arrange a rack about 8 inches below the heat source and turn on the heat. If you have a broiler and it has more than one setting, use the low one.

3. If using a head of cauliflower, chop it into small florets. Halve or quarter store-bought florets lengthwise. The chopped florets should be roughly the same size as the uncooked pasta shells. You should have about 4 cups.

4. When the water is boiling, add the pasta and cook according to package directions. With 3 minutes remaining, add the cauliflower florets and boil them with the pasta.

5. Drain the pasta and cauliflower well and return them to the stockpot. Add the marinara sauce and half of the mozzarella cheese. Stir gently to combine.

6. Spray an unlined rimmed baking sheet with nonstick cooking spray and spread the cauliflower and pasta on it in a single layer that reaches to the edges of the pan.

7. Top the pasta evenly with the remaining half of the mozzarella cheese and all the Parmesan cheese. Tear the pancetta into bite-size pieces and scatter them on it.

8. Broil until the cheese bubbles, the pasta has turned golden in spots, and the pancetta becomes crispy, 3 to 7 minutes. Broiler temperatures can vary widely, so watch closely to avoid burning.

9. Tear fresh basil leaves into pieces, garnish, and serve warm.

Roasted Cauliflower and Tahini Soup

The real magic in this dish happens when you stir crunchy homemade croutons into a light yet richly creamy soup. The cauliflower and tahini give the soup its signature savory flavor.

SERVES 4   PREP: 10 MINUTES   COOK: 45 MINUTES   TOTAL: 55 MINUTES

cutting board · knife · large mixing bowl · 2 rimmed baking sheets · parchment paper · large saucepan · blender

1 medium head cauliflower (2 pounds or 12 ounces florets)

¼ cup olive oil, plus more for drizzling

1½ teaspoons kosher salt, more if needed

3 slices sourdough bread

3 cups low-sodium vegetable stock, plus up to 1 more cup as needed

1 large lemon

3 tablespoons tahini

chopped fresh parsley and/or chives for garnish

1. In the oven, arrange a rack in the lower position and another in the upper position. Preheat it to 425°F.

2. If using a head of cauliflower, chop it into florets. Halve store-bought florets lengthwise. You should have about 4 cups.

3. In a large mixing bowl, combine the florets with 2 tablespoons of the olive oil and 1 teaspoon of the salt, coating evenly.

4. On an unlined rimmed baking sheet, spread the cauliflower in an even layer. Roast it on the upper rack until tender and golden in spots, 20 to 30 minutes, stirring halfway through cooking.

5. Meanwhile, cube the sourdough bread into ½-inch cubes. In the same bowl used to dress the cauliflower, combine the bread cubes with the remaining 2 tablespoons of olive oil and ½ teaspoon of salt.

6. On a second unlined rimmed baking sheet, spread the bread cubes in an even layer. Bake them on the lower rack of the oven until crisp and golden, 12 to 18 minutes. Use a hard spatula to flip the croutons halfway through cooking.

7. When the cauliflower has been roasting for 20 minutes, place a large saucepan over medium-high heat. Add the stock and cook until it simmers. Add the roasted cauliflower to the simmering broth and cook until the cauliflower falls apart, about 10 more minutes.

CONTINUES →

8. Meanwhile, squeeze the lemon for 1½ tablespoons of fresh juice.

9. Remove the cauliflower from the heat and stir in the tahini and lemon juice.

10. With an immersion blender or transferring to a countertop blender, blend the soup until smooth.

11. If necessary, add up to 1 more cup of stock to thin the soup to pour easily.

12. Taste and add salt if needed.

13. Divide the soup among serving bowls, top with the croutons, parsley and/or chives, and a drizzle of olive oil.

Cauliflower al Pastor Burrito Bowls

If you want to pack a lot of flavor into cauliflower, coat it in al pastor sauce, which takes inspiration from the sweet-tart, pineapple-based Mexican sauce often served with roast pork. I've served cauliflower al pastor in a variety of ways, including in tacos and on tostadas, but this way tastes best to me. The rice soaks up the sauce, and the other toppings add great color and flavor.

SERVES 4   PREP: 25 MINUTES   COOK: 45 MINUTES   TOTAL: 1 HOUR 10 MINUTES

large saucepan or rice cooker · cutting board · knife · colander · small bowl · large jar · immersion blender or countertop blender · large lidded sauté pan

---

1½ cups uncooked white or brown rice

1 medium head cauliflower (2 pounds or 12 ounces florets)

one 20-ounce can pineapple pieces in juice

3 tablespoons tomato paste

2 cloves garlic

2 teaspoons chili powder

1 teaspoon smoked paprika

½ teaspoon dried oregano

½ teaspoon kosher salt

black pepper

1 small white onion

1 tablespoon cooking oil

one 15½-ounce can pinto beans

1 lime

1 avocado

fresh cilantro for garnish

tortilla chips for serving (optional)

sour cream or Miso Cashew Cream (page 9) for serving

1. On the stovetop or using a rice cooker, cook the rice according to package directions.

2. If using a head of cauliflower, chop it into small florets. Halve store-bought florets lengthwise. You should have about 4 cups.

3. Drain the pineapple juice into a small bowl, reserving the juice and the pieces.

4. In a jar, combine ¾ cup of pineapple juice and 1 cup of pineapple pieces. Reserve the remaining pineapple pieces. Use any remaining juice for another recipe or purpose.

5. To the jar of juice and pieces, add the tomato paste, garlic cloves, chili powder, smoked paprika, oregano, salt, and a few twists of black pepper. Blend with an immersion blender or transfer to a countertop blender and blend until smooth.

6. Dice the onion, reserving ¼ cup for topping.

7. In a large lidded sauté pan over medium heat, add the cooking oil and the diced onion. Cook, stirring often, until the onions become translucent, 4 to 6 minutes.

8. Add the sauce and bring to a simmer. Add the reserved pineapple pieces and cauliflower and stir to coat evenly. Cover and cook for 8 minutes.

CONTINUES →

9. Remove the lid and continue cooking, stirring occasionally, until the florets become tender and the sauce has thickened, about 10 more minutes.

10. Meanwhile, drain and rinse the pinto beans and warm them in the microwave or on the stovetop. Slice the lime and avocado.

11. When ready to serve, set out the rice, avocado and lime, pinto beans, cilantro leaves, and reserved diced onion. Assemble the bowls, buffet style, at the table.

12. Serve with tortilla chips for scooping if desired.

Kung Pao Cauliflower

The star of this dish is the savory, spicy kung pao sauce with lots of peanuts for crunch. Cauliflower plays along, proving that it easily can stand in for meat in any take-out, fake-out-style meal.

SERVES 2   PREP: 20 MINUTES   COOK: 35 MINUTES   TOTAL: 55 MINUTES
large saucepan or rice cooker • cutting board • knife • small bowl or jar • large lidded sauté pan

1½ cups uncooked long grain rice

1 medium head cauliflower (2 pounds or 12 ounces florets)

1½-inch piece fresh ginger, peeled

2 cloves garlic

4 stalks green onions

5 tablespoons hoisin sauce

3 tablespoons low-sodium soy sauce or tamari

2 tablespoons rice vinegar

2 tablespoons ketchup

½ teaspoon crushed red pepper flakes

¼ cup water

¾ teaspoon kosher salt

½ cup roasted, unsalted peanuts

1. On the stovetop or using a rice cooker, cook the rice according to package directions.

2. If using a head of cauliflower, chop it into florets. Halve store-bought florets lengthwise. You should have about 4 cups.

3. Mince the ginger and garlic and thinly slice the green onions.

4. In a small bowl or jar, whisk or shake together the garlic, ginger, hoisin sauce, soy sauce, rice vinegar, ketchup, and crushed red pepper flakes.

5. In a large lidded sauté pan over medium-high heat, whisk together the water and salt. As soon as the water simmers, add the florets and cover the pan. Cook, covered, until the cauliflower edges become tender but the stems remain firm, 4 to 7 minutes.

6. Remove the lid and continue cooking until all the water evaporates, 2 to 3 more minutes.

7. Pour the sauce over the cauliflower and cook, stirring often, until the sauce reduces by roughly half and coats the cauliflower.

8. Remove the pan from the heat and gently stir in the peanuts and green onions.

9. Serve over rice.

Curried Chickpea and Cauliflower Burgers

Get ready for a veggie burger experience like no other. Not only do the burger patties pack a flavorful punch, but the roasted cauliflower binds them together so well that you don't need an egg. As with all veggie burgers, texture matters, so don't skip the crunchy cucumbers and mild lettuce that round out these burgers so well.

SERVES 4   PREP: 30 MINUTES   COOK: 45 MINUTES   TOTAL: 1 HOUR 15 MINUTES
cutting board • knife • rimmed baking sheet • parchment paper • food processor • large mixing bowl • largest nonstick pan • toaster

1 medium head cauliflower (2 pounds or 12 ounces florets)

2 tablespoons cooking oil

1 teaspoon mild curry powder

½ teaspoon kosher salt

1½-inch piece fresh ginger, peeled

one 15½-ounce can chickpeas

⅓ cup rolled or old-fashioned oats

black pepper

¼ cup fresh cilantro

4 ounces seedless cucumber, such as English

½ cup mayonnaise

2 tablespoons sweet or hot mango chutney, such as Patak's

4 hamburger buns

8 leaves mild lettuce, such as butter or Boston

1. Preheat the oven to 425°F.

2. If using a head of cauliflower, chop it into small florets. Halve store-bought florets lengthwise. You should have about 4 cups.

3. In a large mixing bowl, combine the florets with 1 tablespoon of the oil, the curry powder, and ¼ teaspoon of the salt, coating evenly.

4. Line a rimmed baking sheet with parchment paper and spread the cauliflower on it in an even layer. Roast until it becomes tender and golden in spots, 20 to 30 minutes, stirring halfway through cooking.

5. Meanwhile, mince the ginger and drain and rinse the chickpeas.

6. In a food processor, combine the chickpeas, oats, ginger, the remaining ¼ teaspoon of salt, and a few twists of black pepper. Pulse until the chickpeas reduce to roughly a quarter of their original size.

7. When the cauliflower finishes cooking, add it and the cilantro to the food processor and pulse again, scraping down the sides as needed, until everything combines evenly and the pieces of chickpeas and cauliflower are similar sizes.

CONTINUES →

8. Lightly oil your hands and shape the mixture into 4 patties, pressing them firmly so the ingredients stick together.

9. In your largest nonstick pan over medium-low heat, add the remaining 1 tablespoon of cooking oil and the patties. Cook them until the bottoms turn a deep golden brown, 6 to 8 minutes.

10. Flip and cook them on the other side for 6 to 8 more minutes.

11. While the patties cook, thinly slice the cucumbers. Stir together the mayonnaise and chutney. Toast the hamburger buns.

12. Spread the chutney mayo on both sides of the buns. Fill them with the lettuce leaves, cucumber slices, and burger patties.

NOTES: Veggie burgers usually hold together better if they've rested in the fridge long enough for the moisture to equalize from the wet ingredients to the dry ones. If you can, make them ahead of time, cover, and refrigerate for up to 3 days. They also freeze well for up to 3 months. Slowly cooking them maximizes the golden-brown color and crisps the exterior while giving the centers time to heat through.

VARIATION

To make it vegan, use any vegan mayonnaise or Miso Cashew Cream (page 9) where the recipe calls for mayonnaise.

Cauliflower Steak Frites

WITH MUHAMMARA

A sneak peek of this vegan play on steak and fries garnered more Instagram comments than any other recipe photos I've shared. Muhammara, a sauce of roasted bell pepper and walnuts that originated in Syria, makes this dish feel deliciously indulgent.

SERVES 4   PREP: 40 MINUTES   COOK: 35 MINUTES   TOTAL: 1 HOUR 15 MINUTES

large mixing bowl • cutting board • knife • 2 rimmed baking sheets • parchment paper • small bowl • food processor

---

1½ pounds russet potatoes

1 cup walnut halves or ¾ cup walnut pieces

2 medium heads cauliflower (2 pounds or 12 ounces florets)

6 tablespoons cooking oil

2¼ teaspoons kosher salt

1 teaspoon paprika

½ teaspoon ground coriander

½ teaspoon ground turmeric

black pepper

1 small lemon

one 16-ounce jar roasted red peppers, drained

2 tablespoons olive oil

2 cloves garlic

1 teaspoon pomegranate molasses, honey, maple syrup, or agave syrup

chopped fresh parsley or chives for garnish

1. In the oven, arrange a rack in the lower position and another in the upper position. Preheat it to 425°F.

2. While the oven is heating, fill a large mixing bowl with lukewarm water.

3. Slice the potatoes into matchsticks, no more than ¼ inch at their thickest. Transfer each set of raw fries to the water immediately after slicing.

4. Let the raw fries soak for at least 15 and up to 40 minutes.

5. Meanwhile, toast the walnuts. On an unlined rimmed baking sheet, spread the walnuts in an even layer.

6. On the upper rack of the oven, toast the walnuts until they lightly brown and become fragrant, 3 to 5 minutes. Shake them halfway through to prevent scorching. Transfer to a plate to cool. Keep the baking sheet nearby for the cauliflower.

7. While the walnuts are toasting, remove the outer leaves from the cauliflower and discard. If the heads have long stems, slice them off but keep the core intact.

8. Place each head of cauliflower stem side down on a cutting board and slice it into ¾-inch-thick slices. You want 4 to 6 intact "steaks" and a bunch of smaller florets.

9. Line the baking sheet that you used for the walnuts with parchment paper. Add the cauliflower "steaks" in a single layer. Transfer the florets to a mixing bowl.

CONTINUES →

10. In a small bowl, whisk together 4 tablespoons of the cooking oil, 1 teaspoon of the salt, the paprika, coriander, turmeric, and a few twists of black pepper. Brush the tops of the cauliflower steaks generously with the flavored oil. Toss the florets with any remaining flavored oil and scatter them around the steaks. Set the cauliflower aside while you prepare the fries.

11. Drain the water from the bowl of potatoes. Refill it with fresh water and gently swirl the potatoes to remove any excess starch. Drain again and, with paper towels or a clean dish towel, gently pat them very dry.

12. Toss the fries with the remaining 2 tablespoons of cooking oil and 1 teaspoon of salt, coating evenly.

13. On an unlined rimmed baking sheet, spread the seasoned potatoes in an even layer.

14. Bake both the cauliflower and the potatoes until both become tender and golden, 25 to 30 minutes, rotating the pans and gently turning the fries with a hard spatula halfway through cooking.

15. Meanwhile, make the muhammara. Squeeze the lemon for 1 tablespoon of fresh juice.

16. In a food processor, process the toasted walnuts, drained red peppers, olive oil, garlic, lemon juice, pomegranate molasses, and ¼ teaspoon of salt until smooth. Divide the muhammara among four serving plates.

17. On each plate, place 1 cauliflower steak, ¼ of the florets, and ¼ of the fries. Garnish with chopped herbs.

NOTES: When slicing the cauliflower heads, it's OK if some outer florets fall off. Roast them alongside the steaks. Even if the cauliflower doesn't cooperate, it will taste delicious.

Made ahead of time, muhammara will stay fresh for up to 1 week in the refrigerator. Any leftovers work great as a sandwich spread or as a dip for pita and raw or roasted vegetables.

Bell Peppers

Denver Omelet Wrap

When you want a hearty breakfast that uses only one pan, make a quick breakfast egg wrap. Fry an egg and press a tortilla onto it. The cooking egg sticks to the tortilla so you can flip it all over and cook the tortilla until golden and crisp. This version of that great breakfast hack features bell peppers and other fillings to make a satisfying breakfast or light lunch for two.

SERVES 2   PREP: 15 MINUTES   COOK: 10 MINUTES   TOTAL: 25 MINUTES
cutting board • knife • small mixing bowl • large nonstick pan • soft spatula • hard spatula

---

2 ounces deli ham

1 bell pepper or 8 mini sweet bell peppers

¼ small red onion

4 eggs

¾ teaspoon kosher salt

black pepper

1 tablespoon cooking oil

2 tablespoons salted butter

4 burrito-size flour tortillas

2 ounces shredded Cheddar cheese (½ cup)

½ cup baby spinach (optional)

1. Dice the ham, bell pepper, and onion.

2. In a small mixing bowl, whisk the eggs with ¼ teaspoon of the salt and a few twists of black pepper.

3. In a large nonstick pan over medium heat, add the cooking oil, the peppers, onions, and the remaining ½ teaspoon of salt. Cook, stirring occasionally, until the peppers and onions become tender and golden brown in spots, 5 to 6 minutes.

4. Add the ham and cook until it warms through, about 2 more minutes.

5. Transfer the vegetables and ham to a plate or bowl.

6. Return the pan to the heat, and melt 1 tablespoon of the butter, swirling to coat the bottom. Pour half of the whisked eggs into the pan and cook, stirring occasionally until the eggs are nearly set, 2 to 3 minutes. When the eggs are nearly set, use a soft spatula to move the eggs gently into a round shape slightly smaller than the tortillas.

7. Top the eggs with a tortilla and cook for 1 more minute so the eggs stick to the tortilla.

8. With a hard spatula, gently flip the egg and tortilla so the egg is on top. Top it with half of the cheese, half of the spinach, and half of the bell pepper mixture. Cook until the egg whites set and the tortilla turns golden brown, 2 to 3 more minutes. When done, transfer it to a plate.

CONTINUES →

VARIATION

To make it vegetarian, use ½ cup of drained and rinsed black beans instead of the ham.

9. Repeat steps 6 through 8 with the remaining ingredients.

10. Roll the tortillas and serve warm.

TIP Make these wraps ahead of time, wrap them tightly in foil, and refrigerate for up to 2 days or freeze for up to 3 months. If frozen, thaw in the refrigerator overnight and reheat in the oven, still in the foil, at 425°F for 20 minutes.

Cajun Honey Salmon Bites

WITH MINI SWEET PEPPERS

This dish offers a great way to use mini sweet peppers, which will brighten any meal. Nothing balances the spiciness of Cajun seasoning like a honey butter sauce. This is delicious served over creamy polenta, but pasta, rice, or any other grain work just as well.

SERVES 4   PREP: 15 MINUTES   COOK: 40 MINUTES   TOTAL: 55 MINUTES

medium saucepan · cutting board · knife · mixing bowl · large nonstick pan · serving platter or shallow bowl

---

1 cup uncooked polenta

1 pound mini sweet peppers

4 green onions

1½ pounds salmon, skin removed

¼ cup cooking oil

1 tablespoon Cajun or jerk seasoning, mild or spicy

2 teaspoons red wine vinegar

¼ teaspoon kosher salt

1 large lemon

3 tablespoons salted butter

1 teaspoon honey

1. Cook the polenta according to package directions.

2. While the polenta cooks, slice the bell peppers crosswise into ¼-inch slices. Discard the stems but don't worry about the cores or seeds. Thinly slice the green onions.

3. Cut the salmon into 1-inch cubes and transfer them to a mixing bowl.

4. To the salmon, add 1 tablespoon of the cooking oil, the Cajun seasoning, and red wine vinegar. Stir gently to coat evenly.

5. In your largest nonstick pan over medium-high heat, heat 1 tablespoon of the cooking oil and add the bell peppers and salt. Cook, stirring often, until the peppers become tender, 4 to 6 minutes.

6. When the polenta has finished cooking, transfer it to a large serving platter or shallow bowl and cover to keep it warm.

7. Spread the cooked peppers on the polenta and cover again.

8. Reduce the heat to medium and add the remaining 2 tablespoons of cooking oil to the pan, followed by the salmon in a single layer. Work in batches if necessary, adding additional oil if the pan dries out. Cook until the salmon turns golden brown on one side and releases easily from the pan, about 2 minutes.

CONTINUES →

9. Flip the salmon and cook on all sides until it becomes tender and flakes easily with a fork, 2 to 4 more minutes. Add the salmon to the polenta and cover again.

10. Meanwhile, juice the lemon for 1½ tablespoons of fresh juice.

11. Add the butter to the pan and deglaze any browned bits as it melts. When the butter has melted and is bubbling, remove the pan from the heat and whisk in the lemon juice, honey, and green onions.

12. Pour the butter sauce over the salmon, peppers, and polenta and serve warm.

TIPS You can ask the person at your seafood counter to remove the salmon skin for you.
Check your Cajun or jerk seasoning to make sure it includes salt. If not, add an extra ½ teaspoon of kosher salt when you add the seasoning.

VARIATION

To make it vegetarian, use 12 ounces of thinly sliced portobello mushrooms instead of the salmon. The mushrooms need to cook a few more minutes than the fish, so don't rush those steps.

Roasted Bell Peppers

Use peppers of any color with this method for tender, subtly smoky results.

YIELD VARIES   PREP: 5 MINUTES   COOK: 18 MINUTES   TOTAL: 23 MINUTES
rimmed baking sheet • aluminum foil • cutting board • knife • bowl

---

1 tablespoon cooking oil

bell peppers

1. Preheat the oven to 450°F.

2. Line a rimmed baking sheet with foil and brush it with the cooking oil.

3. Halve the bell peppers lengthwise, core them, and seed them.

4. Place the pepper halves, cut sides down, on the prepared baking sheet and bake until the skins blacken in many spots and the peppers soften, 20 to 25 minutes.

5. Transfer the peppers to a bowl and cover it tightly with foil or a lid. Let the peppers rest until they become cool enough to handle, at least 10 minutes.

6. Carefully remove and discard the peels and stems. Don't run the peppers under water to remove the skins, which will wash away the smoky flavor.

NOTE: In an airtight container in the fridge, the roasted peppers will keep for up to 1 week.

Bell Pepper, Potato, and Sausage Bake

This dish resembles a potato hash, but because it's a bake you don't need to stand over the stove and stir it. The sausage, whether meat-based or vegetarian, flavors the other ingredients as it cooks.

SERVES 4   PREP: 10 MINUTES   COOK: 40 MINUTES   TOTAL: 50 MINUTES

cutting board · knife · large mixing bowl · rimmed baking sheet · hard spatula · nonstick pan

---

2 bell peppers

1½ pounds small red potatoes

1 small red onion

¼ cup olive oil

1 teaspoon kosher salt, plus more for the eggs

black pepper

12 ounces Soyrizo, vegetarian sausage, or chicken apple sausage

4 large eggs

hot sauce for serving (optional)

1. Preheat the oven to 400°F.

2. Halve the bell peppers lengthwise, core them, and stem them. Slice the peppers into bite-size pieces. Quarter the potatoes and chop the onion.

3. In a large mixing bowl, combine the prepared vegetables with 2 tablespoons of the olive oil, the salt, and a few twists of black pepper. Stir to coat evenly.

4. On an unlined rimmed baking sheet, spread the vegetables in an even layer and roast them for 20 minutes.

5. Meanwhile, in the same bowl used for the vegetables, prepare the sausage. If using Soyrizo, crumble it directly into the bowl. If using vegetarian or chicken apple sausage, slice it first. Add 1 tablespoon of the olive oil and stir to combine.

6. After the veggies have roasted for 20 minutes, use a hard spatula to flip all the ingredients on the sheet. Spread the sausage evenly on the roasted veggies and return the sheet to the oven. Continue roasting until a fork easily pierces the potatoes, 15 to 20 more minutes.

7. About 5 minutes before the vegetables and sausage have finished roasting, place a large nonstick pan over medium heat and add the remaining 1 tablespoon of oil.

8. Crack the 4 eggs in the hot oil and season with salt and black pepper to taste. Cook until the whites nearly set, 1 to 2 minutes. Cover the pan and remove it from the heat while the eggs finish cooking.

9. Divide the vegetables and sausage among four serving plates. Top each portion with a fried egg and serve.

Red Pepper Soup

WITH ROASTED CHICKPEAS

Chickpeas give this slightly smoky soup a creamy texture without needing cream or other dairy. While you make the soup, roasting more chickpeas in spices creates a perfect crunchy topping for each bowl.

SERVES 4   PREP: 20 MINUTES   COOK: 30 MINUTES   TOTAL: 50 MINUTES
paper towel or clean dish towel • large mixing bowl • rimmed baking sheet • cutting board • knife • large saucepan • immersion or countertop blender

---

¼ cup canned chickpeas

¼ teaspoon kosher salt, more if needed

3 red Roasted Bell Peppers (page 88) or from a 16-ounce jar

1 clove garlic

1 small white or yellow onion

1 tablespoon oil from a jar of sun-dried tomatoes, plus more for topping

4 cups low-sodium vegetable stock

½ cup packed sun-dried tomatoes

2 teaspoons apple cider vinegar

1 pinch granulated white sugar, if needed

1 batch Roasted Chickpeas (page 6)

chopped fresh parsley, chives, or basil for garnish

1. Drain and rinse the ¼ cup of chickpeas. Rub them gently in a paper towel or clean dish towel to dry. Discard any skins that fall off in the process.

2. If using jarred bell peppers, drain them. Dice the garlic and onion.

3. In a large saucepan over medium heat, heat the oil from the jar of sun-dried tomatoes and add the onion, garlic, and ¼ teaspoon of salt. Cook, stirring frequently, until the onion becomes translucent, 4 to 6 minutes.

4. To the saucepan, add the vegetable stock, ¼ cup of chickpeas, sun-dried tomatoes, and roasted red peppers (whole). Simmer gently, adjusting the heat as needed, for 10 minutes.

5. Stir the vinegar into the soup. Blend the soup with an immersion blender or transfer to a countertop blender and blend until smooth.

6. Taste and adjust the seasoning if necessary. If the flavors taste flat, add salt. If it already tastes salty enough, try a pinch of granulated white sugar, which will highlight the natural sweetness of the peppers and tomatoes.

7. Divide the soup among four serving bowls. Top each bowl with Roasted Chickpeas, fresh herbs, and a drizzle of oil from the jar of sun-dried tomatoes.

Ginger Garlic Lettuce Wraps

Tons of aromatics pack these refreshing lettuce wraps with crisp texture and flavor. Use lean ground beef, 90 percent lean or higher, so you don't have to drain the meat in the middle of cooking.

SERVES 4   PREP: 15 MINUTES   COOK: 40 MINUTES   TOTAL: 55 MINUTES
medium saucepan or rice cooker • cutting board • knife • small bowl or jar • wok or nonstick skillet

---

1½ cup uncooked white or brown rice

2 red bell peppers

3 cloves garlic

1½-inch piece fresh ginger, peeled

⅔ cup water

¼ cup low-sodium soy sauce or tamari

1 tablespoon cornstarch

2 tablespoons packed brown sugar

2 tablespoons hoisin sauce

1 tablespoon rice vinegar

½ teaspoon red pepper flakes

1 tablespoon cooking oil

1½ pounds lean ground beef

2 teaspoons white sesame seeds

16 large leaves lettuce, such as bibb, Boston, or butter

½ cup roasted, unsalted peanuts

hot sauce for serving (optional)

1. On the stovetop or using a rice cooker, cook the rice according to package directions.

2. Dice the bell peppers and mince the garlic and ginger.

3. In a small bowl or jar, whisk or shake together the water and soy sauce. Add the cornstarch and whisk or shake until no dry spots remain. Add the ginger, brown sugar, hoisin sauce, rice vinegar, and red pepper flakes and whisk or shake to combine.

4. In a wok or large nonstick skillet over medium-high heat, heat the cooking oil and add the bell peppers and garlic. Cook until the vegetables become fragrant and start to soften, 3 to 4 minutes.

5. Add the ground beef and cook, breaking the beef apart, until it mostly cooks through but remains pink in a few spots, about 8 minutes.

6. Stir or shake the sauce one more time and pour it over the beef. Cook, stirring occasionally, until the sauce thickens and coats the meat and vegetables, 3 to 4 minutes.

7. Transfer the meat to a serving bowl and top it with the sesame seeds.

8. Set out the lettuce leaves, cooked rice, beef, roasted peanuts, and hot sauce (if using), buffet style. Assemble the wraps at the table as you eat them.

 TIP Prep this meal ahead of time. Cook and organize all the components and store them separately in the fridge. Warm the filling and the rice in the microwave right before serving.

VARIATION

To make it vegetarian, use tofu instead of ground beef. Drain 16 ounces of extra-firm tofu well. Crumble it on a paper towel or a clean, dry dish towel and pat dry. Cook the crumbled tofu until dry, 5 to 8 minutes, browning it in spots, before adding the sauce.

Black Bean Smash Burgers

WITH ROASTED RED PEPPER SALSA

These smash burgers run thin, which means they become crispy and lacy around the edges as they cook. You need just ⅓ cup of cooked quinoa, so this recipe puts smaller amounts of leftovers to good use—or just make a small batch of quinoa before you start. Smaller patties mean plenty of room for the tangy, tart salsa. Like any great smash burger, these include a special sauce.

SERVES 4   PREP: 25 MINUTES   COOK: 30 MINUTES   TOTAL: 55 MINUTES
small saucepan · colander · medium mixing bowl · pastry blender or potato masher · cutting board · knife · 2 small bowls · griddle or large skillet

2 tablespoons uncooked quinoa or ⅓ cup cooked quinoa

one 15½-ounce can black beans

1½ teaspoons paprika

½ teaspoon ground cumin

½ teaspoon kosher salt

black pepper

1 egg

⅓ cup panko bread crumbs

1 shallot

1 red Roasted Bell Pepper (page 88) or from a jar

2 teaspoons capers

¼ cup mayonnaise

2 teaspoons Dijon mustard

¼ teaspoon garlic powder

4 hamburger buns

1 tablespoon cooking oil

2 ounces baby arugula (2 cups)

1. If using uncooked quinoa, fill a small saucepan halfway with water and, over medium-high heat, bring it to a boil. Add the quinoa and simmer until it becomes tender and fluffy, about 20 minutes. Drain well and set aside to cool.

2. Drain and rinse the black beans. Transfer them to a medium mixing bowl and add 1 teaspoon of the paprika, the cumin, salt, and a few twists of black pepper. With a pastry blender or potato masher, mash the beans and spices until the mixture becomes sticky and only small bits of bean remain intact.

3. Add the egg, panko, and cooked quinoa and mix well.

4. Let the bean mixture sit at room temperature for at least 10 minutes and up to 30 minutes so the moisture equalizes from the wet ingredients to the dry ones, which will help the patties hold their shape.

5. Meanwhile, make the salsa. Finely dice the shallot and the roasted red pepper.

6. In a small bowl, combine the shallot, roasted red pepper, and the capers.

7. In another small bowl, combine the mayo, mustard, the remaining ½ teaspoon of the paprika, and the garlic powder.

CONTINUES →

8. With lightly oiled hands, divide the bean mixture into four equal portions and flatten them into patties that will fit inside the hamburger buns.

9. Heat a griddle or your largest skillet over medium heat. Brush it with the oil and add the patties, leaving some space among them. Cook the patties on one side until golden brown, 3 to 4 minutes, then flip and cook on the other side for 3 to 4 more minutes.

10. Meanwhile, use the broil function of a toaster oven to toast the insides of the hamburger buns.

11. Spread the bottom halves of the buns with the mayo sauce. Top with arugula and a burger patty. Use a slotted spoon to add a dollop of roasted red pepper salsa and then add the top of the bun.

NOTE: You can make the burger patties ahead of time. Refrigerate them in an airtight container for up to 3 days or freeze them for up to 3 months.

Zucchini

Summer Squash Toast
WITH GOAT CHEESE

In late summer, this is my favorite way to cook zucchini. Adding it to toast with a generous spread of soft goat cheese makes a delicious lunch or light dinner during warm weather. Add a fried egg on top, a sprinkle of Hot Honey Granola (page 10), or a lemony arugula salad on the side for a little something extra.

MAKES 4 TOASTS   PREP: 5 MINUTES   COOK: 15 MINUTES   TOTAL: 20 MINUTES
cutting board · knife · large nonstick pan · mixing bowl

6 ounces goat cheese

1 pound zucchini or yellow summer squash

1 shallot

¼ cup olive oil, more if needed

4 thick slices of bread

½ teaspoon kosher salt

2 teaspoons red wine vinegar

10 leaves fresh basil

black pepper

1. Bring the goat cheese to room temperature so it softens to a spreadable consistency.

2. Halve the squash lengthwise and cut each half into ½-inch semicircles. Dice the shallot.

3. In your largest nonstick pan over medium heat, heat 2 tablespoons of the olive oil and cook the bread on both sides until golden brown, about 4 minutes total. Work in batches if necessary, adding additional olive oil if the pan dries out. Plate the toasted bread.

4. Add the remaining 2 tablespoons of olive oil to the pan and then add the zucchini. Brown it well on one side before flipping it and continuing to cook until it becomes tender and starts to break down, 7 to 10 minutes total.

5. Sprinkle the salt on the cooked squash, add the shallots and vinegar, and stir. Continue cooking for 1 more minute.

6. Remove the pan from the heat. Tear or chop any large basil leaves and stir them into the zucchini.

7. Spread equal amounts of the softened goat cheese on each slice of toast. Use a slotted spoon to transfer the squash to the toast.

8. Season the toast with a few twists of black pepper and serve warm or at room temperature.

Antipasto Zucchini Salad

WITH SWEET BASIL VINAIGRETTE

If you've never eaten zucchini or summer squash raw, you should try it. The delightfully crunchy texture and fresh flavor—no cooking required!—of this summery salad will surprise you. If your grocery store has an olive bar, buy the exact amount of olives and pepper drops that you need. Otherwise, you should be able to find them shelved near the jars of roasted red peppers.

SERVES 4 TO 6   PREP: 20 MINUTES   TOTAL: 20 MINUTES
cutting board · knife · large mixing or serving bowl · small bowl or jar · blender

---

12 ounces zucchini and/or yellow summer squash

10 ounces crisp greens, such as Romaine, green leaf, or little gem lettuce

4 ounces salami

1 cup pitted kalamata olives

½ cup sweet and tangy pepper drops or 5 sweet pickled peppers, such as Peppadew

one 8-ounce container mozzarella pearls

½ cup olive oil

¼ cup white wine vinegar

2 teaspoons honey

1 teaspoon Dijon mustard

½ teaspoon kosher salt

½ cup packed fresh basil leaves

¼ cup toasted pine nuts

black pepper

1. Cut the zucchini into 2½ cups of ½-inch cubes. Chop or shred the lettuce. Combine them in a large mixing or serving bowl.

2. Slice the salami, olives, and peppers if using whole instead of drops. Drain the mozzarella pearls.

3. In a small bowl or jar, combine the olive oil, vinegar, honey, mustard, salt, and basil leaves. With an immersion blender or transferred to a countertop appliance, blend the mixture until only tiny flakes of basil remain.

4. Pour half of the dressing over the lettuce and zucchini and toss gently to combine. Scatter the salami, olive, peppers, and mozzarella over the top. Drizzle with more dressing to preference.

5. Top the salad with pine nuts and a few twists of black pepper before serving.

 TIP If you don't use all the dressing, it makes a fantastic dressing for pasta salad, or you can drizzle it over sliced tomatoes and mozzarella.

VARIATION

To make it vegetarian, replace the salami with 1 can of drained and rinsed white beans.

Summer Squash Minestrone

The rind of Parmesan cheese contains flavor gold. Even a small cube adds rich, savory notes to this quick-cooking, classic Mediterranean soup.

SERVES 4   PREP: 15 MINUTES   COOK: 18 MINUTES   TOTAL: 33 MINUTES
cutting board • knife • large saucepan

12 ounces zucchini and/or yellow summer squash

3 cloves garlic

one 15½-ounce can white beans

3-inch chunk Parmesan cheese, with rind

2 tablespoons olive oil, plus more for drizzling

2 tablespoons tomato paste

2 teaspoons Italian seasoning

½ teaspoon kosher salt, more if needed

6 cups low-sodium vegetable stock

one 14-ounce can diced fire-roasted tomatoes, with liquid

1 cup dry ditalini pasta or soup shells

1 small lemon

fresh basil for garnish

1. Cut the zucchini into 2½ cups of ½-inch cubes. Mince the garlic. Drain and rinse the white beans. Finely grate the cheese, reserving the rind.

2. In a large saucepan over medium heat, add the olive oil, tomato paste, zucchini, garlic, Italian seasoning, and salt and sauté until the garlic becomes fragrant, 3 to 4 minutes.

3. Add the stock, tomatoes and liquid, and Parmesan rind. Increase the heat to medium-high. Simmer the soup until the zucchini becomes nearly tender, 4 to 6 minutes.

4. Add the pasta. Simmer until the pasta becomes tender, about 8 more minutes.

5. Meanwhile, squeeze the lemon for 2 teaspoons of fresh juice.

6. Remove the Parmesan rind and discard it. Add the beans and lemon juice and cook until the beans heat through, about 3 minutes.

7. Taste the soup and adjust the seasoning, adding salt if needed.

8. Divide the soup among four serving bowls and top with torn fresh basil and grated Parmesan cheese.

NOTE: If making the soup in advance, cook the pasta separately and stir it into the soup right before serving.

Stuffed Focaccia
WITH ZUCCHINI AND PESTO MAYO

Who doesn't love a giant sandwich? This one eats like a party. The recipe makes a loaf of focaccia brimming with tender zucchini, peppery arugula, and a creamy pesto mayo perfect for spreading and, if you make extra, dipping.

SERVES 6   PREP: 20 MINUTES   COOK: 15 MINUTES   TOTAL: 35 MINUTES

cutting board • knife • large nonstick pan or well-seasoned cast-iron skillet • hard spatula • medium bowl • small bowl

1½ pounds zucchini and/or yellow summer squash

4 shallots

3 tablespoons olive oil

¾ teaspoon salt

2 teaspoons red or white wine vinegar

½ cup mayonnaise

¼ cup pesto

1 loaf focaccia (1 pound) or 1 loaf No-Knead Focaccia (page 246)

3 ounces baby arugula (3 cups)

VARIATION

Focaccia sometimes can prove tricky to find in stores, but another large, bakery-style loaf of bread will work. My No-Knead Focaccia (page 246) is just about the easiest home-made bread you can make. Give it a try!

1. Halve the squash lengthwise and cut the halves into ½-inch slices. Thinly slice the shallots.

2. In your largest nonstick pan or a well-seasoned cast-iron skillet over medium-high heat, add 2 tablespoons of the olive oil and the zucchini. Brown the zucchini well on one side before flipping gently with a hard spatula to brown the other, 8 to 12 minutes total. Transfer the zucchini to a bowl and season it with the salt.

3. Reduce the heat to medium. Add the remaining 1 table-spoon of olive oil and the shallots. Cook, stirring often, until the shallots become tender, 2 to 3 minutes.

4. Pour the vinegar over the shallots and release any browned bits stuck to the bottom of the pan.

5. Transfer the cooked shallots to the bowl of zucchini and stir to combine.

6. Let the zucchini-shallot mixture cool while you make the pesto mayo. In a small bowl, whisk together the mayonnaise and pesto.

7. Halve the focaccia to form two big slices. Toast them, unless very fresh, just until they warm up and the edges turn golden, 4 to 5 minutes.

8. Spread pesto mayo on the insides of the focaccia slices. You may not need to use all the spread.

9. Pile the arugula on the bottom half. Add the zucchini and shallots.

10. Add the top half of the focaccia and press down gently to compact the ingredients. Slice and serve.

Pad Krapow Zucchini

The popular Thai dish pad krapow most often includes chicken or pork. But the savory, spicy sauce and loads of fresh basil work incredibly well with zucchini. Seared in oil until lightly crisp on the outside and tender in the center, zucchini was destined to be stir-fried.

SERVES 2   PREP: 15 MINUTES   COOK: 35 MINUTES   TOTAL: 50 MINUTES

medium saucepan or rice cooker • cutting board • knife • small bowl or jar • large lidded wok or nonstick pan

---

- 1½ cups uncooked white or brown rice
- 1 pound zucchini
- 2 cloves garlic
- 1 to 3 red Fresno chile peppers
- 2 tablespoons low-sodium soy sauce or tamari
- 1 tablespoon hoisin sauce
- 1 tablespoon oyster sauce
- ¼ cup cooking oil
- 30 leaves fresh basil
- 2 large eggs
- kosher salt
- hot sauce, fish sauce, or low-sodium soy sauce/tamari for serving (optional)

1. On the stovetop or using a rice cooker, cook the rice according to package directions.

2. Cut the zucchini into about 3 cups of ½-inch cubes. Mince the garlic and thinly slice the peppers.

3. In a small bowl or jar, whisk or shake together the soy, hoisin, and oyster sauces and garlic.

4. In a large wok or nonstick pan over medium-high heat, add 2 tablespoons of the cooking oil and the zucchini cubes in a single layer. Cook without disturbing until the cubes turn golden brown on the bottom, 2 to 3 minutes.

5. Flip the zucchini and cook until golden brown on a second side, 2 to 3 more minutes.

6. Add the peppers and continue cooking, stirring occasionally until the zucchini has browned on all sides and is nearly tender.

7. Add the sauce and cook, stirring to coat evenly, for 3 to 4 more minutes.

8. Remove the pan from the heat and gently stir in the basil until it wilts. Transfer the zucchini mixture to a serving plate and cover to keep it warm.

9. Wipe the wok or pan and return it to medium-high heat. Add the remaining 2 tablespoons of cooking oil. Crack the eggs in the hot oil and cook until the whites mostly set, with frizzled and golden edges, 2 to 3 minutes.

CONTINUES →

10. Remove the pan from the heat, cover, and let the eggs finish cooking from the residual heat for 1 minute.

11. Divide the rice and zucchini between two serving bowls. Top each bowl with a fried egg and lightly salt.

12. If desired, serve with hot sauce, fish sauce, or more soy sauce at the table.

NOTE: Use Thai basil or holy basil if you can, but Italian basil works just fine, too.

VARIATIONS

Use fewer or more chile peppers depending on spice preference or substitute ¼ to 1 teaspoon of red pepper flakes.

To make it vegetarian, use vegetarian oyster sauce. It contains mushrooms but features the same rich, savory flavor.

Zucchini and Corn Tostadas
WITH GREEN GODDESS SAUCE

Half the fun of tostadas is the messiness of eating them, and these offer no exception. They're packed with bright, fresh vegetable flavor, crunchy texture, and herby notes from the creamy sauce. Woks work well for more than just Asian cooking. Here, using one provides plenty of surface area to brown the zucchini while still retaining some of its crunch.

MAKES 8 TOSTADAS   PREP: 25 MINUTES   COOK: 25 MINUTES   TOTAL: 50 MINUTES

cutting board • knife • small bowl or jar • immersion blender • rimmed baking sheet • oven-safe cooling rack • small saucepan • large wok or nonstick pan

---

3 ears corn or 1¾ cups frozen corn kernels

1 pound zucchini

2 shallots

¾ teaspoon kosher salt

8 corn tortillas

two 16-ounce cans refried beans

¼ cup water

1 teaspoon chili powder

2 tablespoons cooking oil

1 batch Green Goddess Sauce (page 245)

1. Preheat the oven to 400°F.

2. If using ears of corn, shuck and discard the husks. Lay the corn flat on a cutting board and slice off all the kernels. If using frozen, defrost it.

3. Cut the zucchini into 3 cups of ½-inch cubes. Dice the shallots.

4. Top a rimmed baking sheet with an oven-safe cooling rack. Spread the tortillas on the rack in a single layer. Hot air moving underneath them will make them more crunchy, but if you don't have an oven-safe cooling rack, cook the tortillas directly on the baking sheet. Bake, without disturbing, until golden and crisp, 8 to 15 minutes, depending on thickness.

5. In a small saucepan over medium heat, combine the refried beans, water, chili powder, and ¼ teaspoon of salt. Stirring often, bring the mixture to a simmer. When the beans are hot, set them aside and cover them to keep them warm.

6. In a large wok or nonstick pan over medium-high heat, add the cooking oil and the zucchini in a single layer. Cook without disturbing until the zucchini turns golden brown on the bottom, 2 to 3 minutes.

CONTINUES →

7. Flip the zucchini and cook until golden brown on a second side, 2 to 3 more minutes.

8. Add the shallots, corn, and the remaining ½ teaspoon of salt and continue cooking until the zucchini becomes tender but still has some crunch, 2 to 3 more minutes.

9. Assemble the tostadas by topping each tortilla with refried beans, zucchini, and Green Goddess Sauce.

DOUBLE UP!

Make a double batch of Green Goddess Sauce (page 245) and use it for BLAT Salad (page 132) or Green Goddess Grain Bowls with Asparagus and Chicken (page 183).

Zucchini Puff Pastry

WITH RICOTTA AND LEMON

Keep store-bought puff pastry in the freezer, and you can make a simple but show-stopping savory tart any day of the week. This dish makes a great centerpiece for a buffet lunch or a lighter, late-summer dinner. Set it out with a green salad and fresh fruit.

SERVES 4   PREP: 25 MINUTES   COOK: 28 MINUTES   TOTAL: 53 MINUTES
cutting board · knife or mandolin · 3 small bowls · large bowl · rimmed baking sheet · parchment paper

---

1 sheet frozen puff pastry (half of a 17.3-ounce package)

10 ounces zucchini

1 large lemon

¾ teaspoon kosher salt

½ cup whole-milk ricotta cheese

¾ cup freshly grated Parmesan cheese

all-purpose flour for dusting

1 tablespoon olive oil

black pepper

1. Thaw the puff pastry according to package directions.

2. Preheat the oven to 375°F.

3. Slice the zucchini into ⅛-inch discs. A mandolin makes quick work of this step, but a sharp knife and a little extra time also work just fine.

4. Into separate bowls, zest the lemon and squeeze the juice.

5. In a large bowl, add the zucchini slices, lemon juice, and ½ teaspoon of the salt. Stir gently to combine and let the mixture sit at room temperature for 10 minutes.

6. Meanwhile, in a small bowl, stir together the ricotta cheese, ½ cup of the Parmesan cheese, and the remaining ¼ teaspoon salt.

7. Line a rimmed baking sheet with parchment paper and lightly dust a clean, flat surface with flour. Roll out the puff pastry, smoothing any folds or bumps, into a 10-by-12-inch rectangle. Transfer the pastry to the prepared baking sheet.

8. Use a fork to pierce all over the surface of the dough, which will help it bake evenly. Using a sharp knife, score all around the puff pastry, about ½ inch from the edges. Don't cut all the way through the pastry, though; score the top layer just to create a border.

9. Brush the border of the puff pastry with olive oil. Spread the ricotta-Parmesan cheese in a thin layer in the center of the pastry.

CONTINUES →

10. With a clean dish towel or paper towels, press the zucchini dry. Remove as much moisture and salt as possible.

11. Add the zucchini to the pastry, arranging the slices however you like.

12. Top with the remaining ¼ cup of Parmesan cheese, ¼ teaspoon of lemon zest, and a few twists of black pepper.

13. Bake until the edges of the pastry turn golden brown and crisp, 28 to 32 minutes.

14. Let it cool for 5 minutes before slicing. Serve warm or at room temperature. (Leftovers taste great cold, too!)

NOTE: If you have fresh herbs, chop and scatter some on top after the pastry has cooled slightly. Finely chopped basil, dill, or parsley work great here.

Corn

Miso Butter Soba Noodles
WITH CORN AND CHICKEN

This dish has a little bit of everything: sweet pops of corn, earthy noodles, rich miso butter, and tender chicken. The soba noodles make a great base, but if you can't find soba, don't worry. Any other noodle, such as udon, ramen, or even spaghetti, will work just fine.

SERVES 4 PREP: 15 MINUTES COOK: 20 MINUTES TOTAL: 35 MINUTES
stockpot • cutting board • knife • large skillet • mixing bowl • colander

4 ears corn or 2½ cups frozen corn kernels

4 green onions

2 tablespoons cooking oil

¼ teaspoon kosher salt

3 tablespoons salted butter

2 tablespoons low-sodium soy sauce or tamari

3 tablespoons white miso paste

1½ cups shredded cooked chicken

8 ounces soba noodles

2 tablespoons sesame seeds

1. Fill a stockpot half full with water, place it over medium-high heat, and bring it to a boil.

2. Meanwhile, if using ears of corn, shuck and discard the husks. Lay the corn flat on a cutting board and slice off all the kernels. If using frozen, defrost it.

3. Chop the green onions.

4. In a large skillet over medium-high heat, heat the oil and add the corn. Cook until one side turns a deep golden brown and starts to sizzle and pop, 5 to 6 minutes.

5. Add the salt and stir gently to release the kernels from the bottom of the pan.

6. Add the butter, soy sauce, and miso. As the butter melts, scrape the bottom of the pan to release any stuck kernels. Gently mash the miso until evenly distributed.

7. Add the chicken and cook just until it heats through, 2 to 3 minutes.

8. Transfer the corn, chicken, and any sauce to a large mixing bowl.

CONTINUES →

9. By now, the pot of water should be boiling. Cook the soba noodles until tender, 4 to 5 minutes, or follow the package instructions.

10. Reserve ½ cup of the noodle water. Drain the noodles in a colander and rinse them with cool water to remove some of the starch.

11. Add the soba noodles and green onions to the chicken and gently fold everything together. As needed and a little at a time, add the reserved noodle water to loosen the noodles. You may not need all the water.

12. Top the noodles with sesame seeds and serve warm. The corn will settle to the bottom of the bowl, so scoop from the bottom as you serve.

NOTES: Store-bought rotisserie chicken works great in this recipe. Choose any color sesame seeds that you like.

Sheet-Pan Corn and Shrimp Bake

If you love a good shrimp boil, you might love the no-boil version even more. Roasting all the ingredients allows their flavors to caramelize and concentrate instead of dissipating in the cooking water. As with the original, this meal works best if you add ingredients at different times, allowing each to cook just as long as it needs. Best of all, you need only one baking sheet.

SERVES 4   PREP: 15 MINUTES   COOK: 25 MINUTES   TOTAL: 40 MINUTES
cutting board • knife • saucepan • aluminum foil • large mixing bowl • rimmed baking sheet

---

4 ears corn

1½ pounds fingerling potatoes or other small potatoes

12 ounces smoked andouille sausage

1 lemon, plus ½ lemon for serving

2 cloves garlic

1 stick salted butter

2 teaspoons Worcestershire sauce

2 teaspoons Old Bay Seasoning

1 pound peeled and deveined large shrimp

fresh parsley for garnish

½ teaspoon kosher salt

condiments of choice, such as cocktail sauce, sour cream, or more butter, for serving

1. In the oven, arrange a rack in the upper position and pre-heat it to 425°F.

2. Shuck the corn. Using a sharp knife, cut each cob into 2 or 3 smaller pieces. Halve the potatoes lengthwise. Cut the sausage diagonally into ½-inch slices. Into a small bowl, zest the lemon and juice it. Mince or grate the garlic.

3. In a small saucepan over medium heat, melt the butter. Remove the pan from the heat and whisk in the Worcestershire sauce, lemon juice and zest, garlic, and Old Bay Seasoning. Return the pan to low heat so the melted butter stays warm but doesn't bubble.

4. One at a time, place a piece of corn in the center of a small piece of foil. Top it with 1 teaspoon of the butter sauce and wrap it tightly in the foil. Spread the wrapped pieces of corn on an unlined rimmed baking sheet.

5. In a large mixing bowl, combine the potatoes and sausage with 2 tablespoons of butter sauce. Spread the mixture around the corn on the baking sheet. Keep the mixing bowl nearby.

6. Bake the potatoes and sausage until the potatoes become tender and a fork easily pierces them, 15 to 25 minutes, depending on the size of the potatoes. Stir halfway through cooking.

7. Remove the baking sheet from the oven but don't turn it off.

CONTINUES →

8. In the same mixing bowl used for the potatoes and sausage, combine the shrimp with 2 tablespoons of butter sauce.

9. Add the shrimp to the potatoes and sausage and stir gently to combine all the ingredients.

10. Return the sheet to the oven and continue cooking until the shrimp become pink all the way through, 5 to 10 minutes, depending on size.

11. Gently stir the ingredients on the baking sheet to recombine them with the sauce that has dripped to the bottom. Carefully remove the corn pieces from their foil wraps.

12. Season the dish with parsley and salt.

13. Transfer the bake to a large serving platter or serve it on the sheet with the remaining butter sauce and other condiments of choice on the side.

VARIATIONS

Andouille sausage tastes quite spicy, but any smoked or pre-cooked sausage will do just fine in its place.

To make it vegetarian, use any vegetarian or vegan sausage in place of the andouille. In place of the shrimp, use one 15½-ounce can of drained and rinsed chickpeas.

Fusilli Corn Carbonara

Unlike the original Italian carbonara sauce, this sauce doesn't include any egg. Blended sweet corn does the work instead, delivering a fresher and more summery taste, with a hint of sweetness that balances the saltiness of the pancetta and Parmesan.

SERVES 4   PREP: 10 MINUTES   COOK: 35 MINUTES   TOTAL: 45 MINUTES
stockpot · cutting board · knife · skillet · blender

---

kosher salt for the pot

4 ears corn

6 ounces pancetta

1 pound uncooked fusilli corti bucati pasta or other fun shaped pasta

¾ cup water, plus more as needed

2-inch chunk Parmesan cheese

black pepper

1. Fill a stockpot half full with water, place it over medium-high heat, and salt it generously, about 1 tablespoon. Don't worry about measuring but don't skimp. Bring the water to a boil.

2. Meanwhile, shuck the corn and discard the husks. Dice the pancetta, unless it's prediced.

3. In a small skillet over medium heat, add the pancetta and cook it, stirring occasionally, until golden and crisp, about 5 minutes. Transfer to a paper towel–lined plate to drain and cool.

4. The pasta water should be boiling by now. Add the corn cobs and simmer them until bright yellow and tender, 5 to 6 minutes.

5. Use heatproof tongs to remove the corn, leaving the pot of water on the stove and boiling. If any corn silks are floating in the water, use a slotted spoon to remove them.

6. Add the pasta to the boiling corn water and cook according to package directions. Drain well.

7. While the pasta cooks, slice the kernels from the corn cobs. Reserve ½ cup of kernels and add the remaining kernels to a blender with the ¾ cup of water. Blend until smooth, adding additional water if needed to create a smooth, thin sauce.

8. Pour the corn sauce over the pasta and toss gently to combine evenly. Taste and add salt if needed. For naturally sweet corn, you may need a little more salt for balance.

9. Transfer the pasta to a serving bowl or individual serving plates.

10. Grate Parmesan cheese generously on the pasta.

11. Finish the pasta with the reserved corn kernels, pancetta, and a few twists of black pepper.

NOTE: Don't skip salting the pasta water. The pancetta and Parmesan cheese contain plenty of salt, but the corn and the pasta need similar seasoning, as well.

 TIP Look for diced pancetta in the deli section of your grocery store. If they don't have it, ask the deli clerk for help.

Elote Grilled Cheese

Mexican street corn in a crave-worthy sandwich? You'd better believe it! You want to cook these sandwiches low and slow so that the cheese has time to melt while the bread develops a golden, crisp crust. If you've never spread mayonnaise instead of butter on the outside of your grilled cheese, prepare to convert. Mayo has a higher smoke point, which allows the outside of the bread to turn extra golden with less chance of burning.

SERVES 4   PREP: 15 MINUTES   COOK: 30 MINUTES   TOTAL: 45 MINUTES
cutting board · knife · large nonstick pan · large mixing bowl · griddle · hard spatula

---

4 ears corn or 2½ cups frozen corn kernels

10 ounces Monterey Jack cheese

¼ cup cilantro leaves

2 cloves garlic

2 green onions

1 small Jalapeño pepper

2 tablespoons cooking oil

¼ teaspoon kosher salt

1 tablespoon mayonnaise, plus more for the bread

zest of 1 lime

½ teaspoon chili powder

8 slices sandwich bread

1. If using ears of corn, shuck and discard the husks. Lay the corn flat on a cutting board and slice off all the kernels. If using frozen, defrost it.

2. Grate the cheese. You should have about 3 cups.

3. Finely chop the cilantro, garlic, green onions, and Jalapeño pepper.

4. In a large nonstick pan over medium-high heat, heat the cooking oil and add the corn kernels. Cook until they turn deep golden brown on one side and start to sizzle and pop, 6 to 7 minutes.

5. Add the salt, Jalapeño pepper, and garlic and stir gently to release any kernels stuck to the bottom of the pan. Continue cooking until the corn browns all over, about 2 more minutes.

6. Transfer the corn to a large mixing bowl. Add the cheese, green onions, cilantro, 1 tablespoon of mayonnaise, lime zest, and chili powder and stir well.

7. Heat a large griddle over low heat. Thinly spread mayonnaise on one side of all 8 slices of bread. Place the bread mayo-side down on the griddle.

8. Carefully divide the cheesy corn filling among 4 slices of bread. Toast all 8 slices until the cheese starts melting.

9. Flip the 4 empty slices onto the cheese, toasted sides up. Press with a hard spatula.

10. Flip the sandwiches with the spatula a few more times and continue cooking until the cheese melts fully and the bread has a crisp golden crust on both sides. Depending on the thickness of your bread, time will vary. Don't rush it.

Salmon Tacos
WITH CORN AND AVOCADO SALSA

Give each component of this dish the attention it deserves: creamy slaw, flaky salmon, and tangy-crisp salsa. For added flavor and texture, look for a slaw blend instead of the classic cabbage. I love making this recipe with a blend that includes shredded broccoli stems, kale, and/or carrots.

SERVES 4   PREP: 35 MINUTES   COOK: 10 MINUTES   TOTAL: 45 MINUTES
rimmed baking sheet • foil • cutting board • knife • 3 mixing bowls

---

4 ears corn or 2½ cups frozen corn kernels

2 large limes

½ small red onion

1 teaspoon kosher salt

¼ teaspoon honey

¼ cup mayonnaise

4 cups slaw mix

2 tablespoons cooking oil

1 teaspoon ground cumin

½ teaspoon chili powder

¼ teaspoon garlic powder

¼ teaspoon brown sugar (optional)

black pepper

1 pound salmon

1 cup fresh cilantro

2 avocados

12 taco-size corn or flour tortillas

1. If your oven doesn't have a dedicated broiler, use the main compartment. Arrange a rack about 8 inches below the heat source and turn on the heat. Line a rimmed baking sheet with foil.

2. If using ears of corn, shuck and discard the husks. Lay the corn flat on a cutting board and slice off all the kernels. If using frozen, defrost it.

3. Into a small bowl, zest and juice the limes. You should have about 4 tablespoons of lime zest juice. Dice the onion.

4. In a medium mixing bowl, whisk together 2 tablespoons of lime zest juice, ½ teaspoon of the ground cumin, ¼ teaspoon of the salt, and honey. Add the corn kernels and diced onion. Let the mixture marinate at room temperature while you prepare the rest of the dish, up to 30 minutes.

5. In another medium mixing bowl, whisk together 2 tablespoons of lime zest juice, the mayonnaise, and ¼ teaspoon of salt. Add the slaw mix and stir well to coat evenly. Let the slaw marinate at room temperature while you prepare the rest of the dish, up to 30 minutes.

6. In another mixing bowl or baking dish, whisk together the oil, ½ teaspoon salt, ½ teaspoon ground cumin, chili powder, garlic powder, brown sugar, and a few twists of black pepper. Add the salmon and gently turn it to coat all sides with the spice mixture. Place the salmon skin-side down on the prepared baking sheet.

CONTINUES →

7. Broil the salmon until it flakes easily with a fork, 4 to 10 minutes, depending on thickness and broiler heat. Broiling salmon can produce some smoke, so use the oven's hood fan or open a window if you notice any.

8. Meanwhile, chop the cilantro and cube the avocados. Gently stir both into the corn salsa.

9. Warm the tortillas according to package directions.

10. Gently use a fork to flake the salmon to make it easier to put it in tortillas.

11. At the table, fill the tortillas with slaw, salmon, and corn salsa.

NOTE: You can skip the brown sugar, but it creates a nice golden-brown crust on the salmon.

DOUBLE UP!

The rub used on the salmon in this recipe is similar to the stand-alone Dry Rub (page 240). Make a double batch of it to use on Dry-Rub Chicken with Cucumber Peach Salsa (page 136).

Cucumbers

CUCUMBER TOAST
WITH BOURSIN AND DILL   132

CUCUMBER CRUNCH SALAD WITH SESAME
GINGER VINAIGRETTE   135

DRY-RUB CHICKEN WITH
CUCUMBER PEACH SALSA   136

MARINATED CHICKPEAS AND CUCUMBERS
WITH SUN-DRIED TOMATO VINAIGRETTE   139

GREEK SALAD JARS WITH QUINOA
AND PIZZA VINAIGRETTE   140

NO-ROLL SUSHI BOWLS   143

Cucumber Toast

WITH BOURSIN AND DILL

A good fancy toast hits the spot for light lunches, summer dinners, and so much more. Seedless cucumbers add the perfect tang to these crunchy toasts. If you haven't had Boursin cheese before, here's your chance to give it a try. Chances are this herby cheese spread will become a new fridge staple. Few spreads taste better on crackers.

SERVES 4   PREP: 15 MINUTES   COOK: 10 MINUTES   TOTAL: 25 MINUTES
cutting board · knife · medium mixing bowl · griddle or large nonstick pan

---

1½ pounds seedless cucumbers, such as English

4 sprigs fresh dill

6 tablespoons olive oil, more if needed

3 tablespoons apple cider vinegar

1 teaspoon kosher salt

½ teaspoon granulated white sugar

4 large, thick slices dark pumpernickel bread

one 5.2-ounce package Boursin cheese

2 teaspoons white sesame seeds

black pepper

1. If the cucumber skins seem thick, peel them. Otherwise leave the skin on and slice them into ⅛-inch slices. Chop the dill.

2. In a medium mixing bowl, whisk together 3 tablespoons of the olive oil, vinegar, salt, and sugar until the salt and sugar dissolve.

3. Add the cucumbers and dill and stir to coat well. Marinate the cucumbers for at least 10 minutes and up to 24 hours.

4. To a griddle or large nonstick skillet over medium heat, add the remaining 3 tablespoons of olive oil and the bread. Sear the bread on both sides until golden brown, about 4 minutes total. Work in batches if needed, adding more olive oil if the pan dries out. When both sides of each slice have toasted, transfer the bread to serving plates.

5. Spread the top of each slice of bread with Boursin cheese.

6. Use a slotted spoon to transfer the cucumbers from the marinade and divide them evenly among the toasts.

7. Top with sesame seeds and a few twists of black pepper.

 TIP Whisk 1 teaspoon of Dijon mustard into the leftover cucumber marinade, toss 5 ounces of mixed greens in it, and serve alongside the toasts.

VARIATION

Instead of pumpernickel, you can use a dark whole wheat or whole-grain bread.

Cucumber Crunch Salad

WITH SESAME GINGER VINAIGRETTE

This Asian-inspired dish packs a gingery punch and transforms any protein into a colorful, plentiful meal. In the grocery store, look for crispy wontons in the salad section near the croutons.

SERVES 6   PREP: 30 MINUTES   TOTAL: 30 MINUTES
cutting board • knife • large mixing or salad bowl • small bowl or jar

1 pound seedless cucumbers, such as English

4 green onions

½ cup roasted unsalted peanuts

5 ounces baby spinach (4 cups)

5 ounces coleslaw mix (2 cups)

3½ ounces crispy wontons

1 batch Sesame Ginger Vinaigrette (page 243)

1. If the cucumber skins seem thick, peel them. Otherwise leave the skin on and chop them into bite-size pieces.

2. Chop the green onions and peanuts. If the baby spinach leaves are large, also chop them into bite-size pieces.

3. In a large mixing or salad bowl, combine the cucumber, green onions, peanuts, baby spinach, coleslaw mix, and crispy wontons. Don't toss yet.

4. Add the Sesame Ginger Vinaigrette to the salad a little at a time, tossing between each addition, until dressed to your liking. Serve immediately.

DOUBLE UP!

The vinaigrette used in this recipe is nearly the same as Sesame Ginger Vinaigrette (page 243). Make a double batch of it and use it in Kale and Ramen Salad (page 210).

Dry-Rub Chicken

WITH CUCUMBER PEACH SALSA

When summer produce is in full swing, all you need for dinner is something on the grill and a great salsa that celebrates that produce. This salsa stars three ingredients that shine in late summer: cucumbers, peaches, and basil.

SERVES 4   PREP: 20 MINUTES   COOK: 16 MINUTES   TOTAL: 36 MINUTES
cutting board · knife · mixing bowls · grill or large skillet

1 pound seedless cucumbers, such as English

2 peaches

8 leaves fresh basil

1 clove garlic

3 tablespoons olive oil

¼ teaspoon kosher salt

1 tablespoon apple cider vinegar

1 batch Dry Rub (page 240)

1 pound boneless, skinless chicken breast

1 tablespoon cooking oil

VARIATION

To make it vegetarian, use Halloumi cheese instead of chicken. A firm cheese, Halloumi can withstand searing or grilling without melting or losing its shape. Rinse it before adding the dry rub, though, as its brine can taste *very* salty.

1. If the cucumber skins seem thick, peel them. Otherwise leave the skin on. Finely dice the cucumbers and peaches. Chop the basil and grate or mince the garlic.

2. In a small mixing bowl, combine the cucumbers, peaches, basil, garlic, 1 tablespoon of the olive oil, and ¼ teaspoon of the salt. Let the salsa marinate at room temperature until you're ready to eat, giving it a gentle stir once or twice as it sits.

3. In a medium mixing bowl, whisk together the remaining 2 tablespoons of olive oil and the apple cider vinegar with the Dry Rub. Add the chicken, turning it to coat all sides.

4. If grilling the chicken, heat the grill to 400°F and brush the grill grates with the cooking oil. If cooking the chicken on the stove, heat the cooking oil in a large skillet over medium heat.

5. Grill or sear the chicken on both sides until it reaches 165°F in the thickest part, 6 to 8 minutes total.

6. Let the chicken rest, covered, for 10 minutes. Slice it thinly and top with the salsa.

DOUBLE UP!

Make a double batch of this Dry Rub (page 243) and use for Salmon Tacos with Corn and Avocado Salsa (page 128).

Marinated Chickpeas and Cucumbers

WITH SUN-DRIED TOMATO VINAIGRETTE

The longer the chickpeas marinate, the more flavors they absorb from the vinaigrette and the more tender they become. Also, cucumbers and tomatoes classify as fruit, botanically speaking, but adapting the old saw: wisdom is not putting either in a fruit salad.

SERVES 4 PREP: 20 MINUTES, PLUS MARINATING TIME TOTAL: 50 MINUTES
cutting board · knife · medium bowl

---

1 pound cucumbers

two 15-ounce cans chickpeas

1 batch Sun-Dried Tomato Vinaigrette (page 242)

3 ounces feta cheese

2 tablespoons finely chopped dill or parsley

VARIATION

To make it a main dish, serve with your favorite grilled skewers: chicken, shrimp, steak, or a mix of colorful vegetables.

1. If the cucumbers have thick skins, peel them first. If they contain seeds, halve them and remove the seeds. Dice the cucumbers.

2. Drain and rinse the chickpeas and add them to a medium bowl with the cucumbers. Add the Sun-Dried Tomato Vinaigrette and stir well to combine.

3. Refrigerate the marinating veggies for at least 30 minutes and up to 3 days.

4. Just before serving, crumble the feta on the salad and add the herbs. Stir gently.

5. Serve chilled or at room temperature.

DOUBLE UP!

Make a double batch of Sun-Dried Tomato Vinaigrette (page 242) and use it in Pearl Couscous Salad (page 206).

Greek Salad Jars

WITH QUINOA AND PIZZA VINAIGRETTE

This salad substitutes a sturdy bell pepper for the more traditional tomatoes to ensure that the finished dish holds up in the fridge for several days. Assemble the jars in the order specified, chickpeas on the bottom. They'll marinate in the dressing and keep the other ingredients separate until you're ready to enjoy.

SERVES 4   PREP: 30 MINUTES   COOK: 25 MINUTES   TOTAL: 55 MINUTES
medium lidded saucepan · cutting board · knife · small bowl or jar · four 16-ounce jars

1¾ cups low-sodium vegetable stock

1 cup uncooked quinoa

12 ounces cucumbers

1 red bell pepper

½ cup pitted kalamata olives

4 ounces feta cheese

one 15-ounce can chickpeas

1 batch Pizza Vinaigrette (page 241)

1. Add the stock in a medium saucepan over medium-high heat and bring it to a boil.

2. Rinse the quinoa. When the stock is boiling, add the quinoa, reduce the heat to medium-low, and cover. Simmer until the quinoa becomes tender and fluffy, 15 to 20 minutes. Remove the pan from the heat and let it sit, covered, for 10 more minutes.

3. Meanwhile, prepare the vegetables. If the cucumbers have thick skins, peel them first. If they contain seeds, halve them and remove the seeds. Dice the cucumbers and bell pepper. Halve the olives. Cut the feta into ½-inch cubes or crumble it into bite-size pieces.

4. Drain and rinse the chickpeas and divide them among the 16-ounce jars. Divide the Pizza Vinaigrette among the jars, then add the cucumbers, bell pepper, feta, and olives.

5. Fluff the quinoa with a fork and divide it among the jars, pressing down to compact the ingredients.

6. Refrigerate for at least 30 minutes or up to 3 days.

7. To serve, eat straight from the jar or transfer the salads to individual serving bowls and stir gently to combine. Serve chilled or at room temperature.

NOTE: If you don't have or don't want to fuss with jars, you can make this recipe as one large salad instead of single servings.

DOUBLE UP!

Make a double batch of Pizza Vinaigrette (page 241) and pour it on Pizza Salad (page 220).

No-Roll Sushi Bowls

Sushi at home doesn't need to be complicated. Set out all the ingredients and build your own sushi bowls at the table. Serve these with full pieces of nori, like those used to roll sushi, or look for small packs of dried seaweed snacks. Sushi rice often contains a light seasoning of vinegar, sugar, and salt, but here quick-pickled cucumbers provide those flavors.

SERVES 4   PREP: 40 MINUTES   COOK: 20 MINUTES   TOTAL: 1 HOUR

mixing bowls · cutting board · knife · small saucepan with a lid · small bowl or jar · large nonstick pan

---

1 pound cucumbers

3 tablespoons rice vinegar

1 tablespoon cooking oil

1 teaspoon toasted sesame oil

1 teaspoon kosher salt

½ teaspoon honey

1½ cups dry sushi rice

1¾ cups water

3 tablespoons mayonnaise

3 tablespoons gochujang sauce

1 cup plain yogurt

1½ pounds salmon

1 large avocado

black pepper

4 green onions

sesame seeds, furikake, or everything bagel seasoning for garnish

4 large pieces nori or 12 small seaweed snacks

1. If your oven doesn't have a dedicated broiler, use the main compartment. Arrange a rack about 8 inches below the heat source and turn on the heat. If you have a broiler and it has more than one setting, use the low one.

2. Line a rimmed baking sheet with foil.

3. If the cucumber skins seem thick, peel them. Otherwise leave the skin on and thinly slice or dice the cucumber.

4. In a mixing bowl, whisk together the rice vinegar, the cooking oil, the toasted sesame oil, and ½ teaspoon of salt, and the honey. Add the cucumber and stir well to coat evenly. Marinate the cucumbers for at least 20 minutes at room temperature or refrigerate for up to 2 days.

5. Rinse the rice in cold water until the water runs clear. This step can take a minute or two, but don't rush. You need to remove as much surface starch as possible.

6. In a small saucepan over medium-high heat, bring the water to a boil. Add the rice, cover immediately, and reduce the heat to low. Cook, covered, until the rice absorbs the water and becomes tender, about 15 minutes.

7. Remove the rice from the heat and let it steam, still covered, for 10 more minutes.

8. In a small bowl or jar, whisk together the mayonnaise and the gochujang sauce. Set 3 tablespoons of this gochujang mayo aside to use as a glaze for the salmon. To the remaining gochujang mayo in the bowl, whisk in the yogurt (you'll use this to top the bowls).

CONTINUES →

VARIATION

To make it vegetarian, use Pan-Fried Tofu (page 5) instead of salmon.

9. Set the salmon skin-side down on the foil-lined baking sheet. Brush the top of it with the 3 tablespoons of gochujang mayo. Season the top of the fish with ½ teaspoon salt and a few twists of black pepper. Broil the salmon until it is opaque, flakes easily with a fork, and registers 125°F in the thickest part, 6 to 8 minutes. (Note: The salmon itself won't burn, but any gochujang mayo that drips off and onto the foil might, so be sure to turn on the oven fan in case things get smoky.)

10. Slice the avocado and chop the green onions.

11. Divide the rice among four serving bowls. Top with salmon, avocado, cucumbers (including some of the dressing), green onions, gochujang yogurt mixture, and sesame seeds, furikake, or everything bagel seasoning.

12. Serve with nori or seaweed snacks on the side.

13. You can eat the bowls with forks and spoons or chopsticks. Crumble the nori or seaweed over the top or scoop the sushi fillings onto pieces of nori and make hand rolls.

NOTE: A short-grain white rice, sushi rice has a slightly sticky texture after cooking. You can use any type of rice for these bowls, though, so if you'd rather use a white or brown rice that you already have on hand, those will work, too. Just be sure to follow the package instructions for cooking because other types of rice require more water than sushi rice.

DOUBLE UP!

The sauce in this recipe is similar to Gochujang Yogurt Sauce (page 240). Make a double batch and use the sauce to make Green Bean and Ginger Wraps with Chicken (page 172), Sweet Potatoes, Broccoli, and Gochujang Chicken (page 61), or Banh Mi Bowls with Quick-Pickled Carrots (page 25).

Tomatoes

Heirloom Tomato and Herb Salad

WITH RED WINE VINAIGRETTE

When the season for tomatoes reaches its peak, you don't need to do much to make the most of them. This simple salad lets their beauty and flavor shine. Aim for a mix of sizes and colors for the best presentation and taste.

SERVES 6 TO 8   PREP: 15 MINUTES   TOTAL: 15 MINUTES
cutting board · knife · small bowl or jar

1 shallot

2 tablespoons red wine vinegar

2 tablespoons olive oil

¼ teaspoon kosher salt

1 pound large heirloom tomatoes

1 pound cherry or grape tomatoes

¼ cup loosely packed fresh herbs, such as basil, cilantro, dill, and/or parsley

sea salt flakes, such as Maldon, for topping

1. Thinly slice the shallot. In a small bowl or jar, whisk or shake together the shallots, vinegar, olive oil, and salt. Marinate the shallots while you prepare the tomatoes.

2. Cut the heirloom tomatoes into slices or wedges. If any of the cores feel very firm, remove and discard them. Halve the cherry tomatoes. You want a nice variety of colors, sizes, and shapes, so don't worry about making everything even. As you slice them, transfer the tomatoes to a large serving platter.

3. Spoon the shallots and dressing on the tomatoes. Tear the fresh herbs into pieces and sprinkle them on the tomatoes, as well.

4. Finish with flaked sea salt and serve immediately.

> **VARIATION**
>
> To make it a main dish, serve it over whipped ricotta or feta with good crusty bread for dipping. It makes a perfect no-cook meal for when it feels too hot to do anything else.
>
> Try topping this salad with crumbled Hot Honey Granola (page 10) for great unch and a bit of a spicy kick.

One-Pan Orzo
WITH TOMATOES, CORN, AND FETA

This creamy stovetop orzo has bursts of juicy tomatoes and crisp corn in every bite. The rice-shaped pasta absorbs the flavor of the tomatoes, making the entire dish taste like summer.

SERVES 4   PREP: 10 MINUTES   COOK: 20 MINUTES   TOTAL: 30 MINUTES
cutting board • knife • large lidded saucepan

---

3 ears corn or 2 cups frozen corn kernels

2 cups cherry or grape tomatoes

2 shallots

3 tablespoons unsalted butter

½ teaspoon kosher salt

2½ cups low-sodium vegetable broth

1½ cups dry orzo pasta

3 ounces feta cheese

fresh basil for garnish

1. If using ears of corn, shuck and discard the husks. Lay the corn flat on a cutting board and slice off all the kernels. If using frozen, defrost it.

2. Halve the tomatoes lengthwise and dice the shallots.

3. In a large lidded saucepan over medium heat, melt the butter.

4. Add the tomatoes, salt, and shallots. Cook, stirring often, until the vegetables start releasing their juices, 4 to 6 minutes.

5. Add the broth. When the stock is simmering, add the orzo and corn.

6. Cover the saucepan and reduce the heat to medium-low to maintain a gentle simmer. Cook the orzo until tender, 10 to 15 minutes. Remove the lid a few times to stir, focusing on the bottom of the pan, where the pasta likely will stick.

7. Remove the saucepan from the heat and crumble the feta into it. Stir for 1 minute to combine and thicken. It may still seem a bit liquidy, but it will continue to thicken as it sits.

8. Top with basil and serve warm.

Farro Caprese

Chewy, nutty farro gives the classic flavors of a caprese salad some extra substance. This side dish works great for summer meals. Make it ahead to enjoy as a light lunch throughout the week.

SERVES 8   PREP: 15 MINUTES   COOK: 15 MINUTES   TOTAL: 30 MINUTES
stockpot · cutting board · knife · medium mixing bowl · colander

---

1½ teaspoons kosher salt

2 cups cherry or grape tomatoes

20 leaves fresh basil

one 8-ounce container mozzarella pearls

1½ cups uncooked pearled farro (see Notes)

1 batch Balsamic Vinaigrette (page 242)

VARIATION

To make it a main dish, add a can of drained and rinsed white beans for a heartier, more satisfying salad or top it, as is, with grilled salmon, chicken, or vegetable skewers.

1. Fill a stockpot half full with water, place it over medium-high heat, and salt it with about 1½ teaspoons of salt. Don't worry about measuring but also don't skimp. Bring the water to a boil.

2. While waiting for the water to boil, halve the tomatoes lengthwise. Thinly slice the basil and drain the mozzarella pearls. If making the farro ahead of time, see Notes.

3. Rinse the farro well under cool water, then add it to the boiling water. Reduce the heat to medium-low to maintain a gentle simmer and cook, stirring occasionally, until the farro has an al dente bite and chewy texture, 15 to 20 minutes.

4. Drain the farro well and rinse it with cool water to stop the cooking process. Put the farro in a mixing bowl with the Balsamic Vinaigrette and stir well. Allow the farro to cool for at least 10 minutes, stirring once or twice to incorporate the vinaigrette as it cools.

5. Stir the tomatoes, basil, and mozzarella into the farro. Serve at room temperature or chill for up to 1 hour before serving.

NOTES: Pearled farro cooks in about 15 minutes, semi-pearled about 20, and whole farro about 40. Actual cooking time can vary depending on the age of the grain. If you're still unsure, check after 15 minutes and treat it like pasta. It should feel tender but have a pleasant chewy texture.

If making the salad ahead of time, combine the cooked farro and vinaigrette and refrigerate it for up to 3 days. Add the tomatoes, basil, and mozzarella just before serving.

DOUBLE UP!

The ingredients for the vinaigrette in this recipe are the same for Balsamic Vinaigrette (page 242). Make a double batch of it and use it to make Sweet Potato Cobb Salad (page 55).

BLAT Salad

Bacon, lettuce, and tomato . . . here's everyone's favorite summer sandwich in salad form. Avocado and herby Green Goddess Sauce (page 245) bring it all together.

SERVES 4   PREP: 20 MINUTES   COOK: 25 MINUTES   TOTAL: 45 MINUTES

cutting board • knife • small mixing bowl or jar • 2 rimmed baking sheets • parchment paper • food processor or blender • large mixing bowl

---

4 thick slices sandwich bread

1½ pounds tomatoes

1 large or 2 medium avocados, peeled and pitted

2 hearts romaine lettuce

12 strips bacon

½ cup plus 2 tablespoons olive oil

1 batch Green Goddess Sauce (page 245)

VARIATION

To work another veggie into this dish, substitute 2 cups of baby spinach for 1 heart of romaine lettuce.

1. In the oven, arrange a rack in the lower position and another in the upper position. Preheat it to 400°F.

2. While the oven heats, cube the bread and transfer the cubes to a mixing bowl.

3. If using large tomatoes, chop them into bite-size pieces. If the tomatoes are particularly juicy, remove some of the seeds so they don't make the salad soggy. If using cherry tomatoes, just halve them. Roughly chop the lettuce.

4. Line a rimmed baking sheet with parchment paper. Spread the bacon on it in a single layer. Bake on the lower rack of the oven, without turning, until crispy, 15 to 20 minutes.

5. Meanwhile, stir 2 tablespoons of the olive oil into the bread cubes. Spread them on a second unlined baking sheet. Bake on the upper rack of the oven until golden and crisp, 10 to 15 minutes. Stir the croutons halfway through cooking.

6. When the bacon finishes cooking, transfer it to a paper towel–lined plate to drain and cool. Let the croutons cool on the baking sheet.

7. Cube the avocado.

8. In a large mixing bowl, gently stir ¼ cup of the Green Goddess Sauce into the lettuce, coating it evenly. Transfer the lettuce to a large serving plate, salad bowl, or individual serving bowls.

9. Top with the tomatoes, avocados, and croutons. Crumble the bacon over the top. Add additional Green Goddess Sauce to taste. (You may not need all of it.)

DOUBLE UP!

Make a double batch of Green Goddess Sauce (page 245) and use it for Zucchini and Corn Tostadas (page 111) or Green Goddess Grain Bowls with Asparagus and Chicken (page 183).

Chicken Cutlets

WITH BURST CHERRY TOMATOES

The juicier the tomatoes, the saucier the topping for this chicken and pasta dish. The abundance of good cherry and grape tomatoes makes this a perfect meal for late summer, but it's terrific any time of year.

SERVES 4   PREP: 20 MINUTES   COOK: 25 MINUTES   TOTAL: 45 MINUTES

stockpot · cutting board · knife · resealable plastic bag · large nonstick pan or well-seasoned cast-iron skillet

---

1 teaspoon kosher salt, plus more for the pot

4 cups cherry or grape tomatoes

2 cloves garlic

1½ pounds boneless, skinless chicken breasts

2 tablespoons all-purpose flour

1 teaspoon paprika

1 teaspoon Italian seasoning

black pepper

4 tablespoons unsalted butter

1 pound uncooked pasta, any shape

1 teaspoon balsamic vinegar

freshly grated Parmesan cheese for serving

1. Fill a stockpot half full with water, place it over medium-high heat, and salt it generously, about 1 tablespoon. Don't worry about measuring but also don't skimp. Bring the water to a boil.

2. Meanwhile, slice the tomatoes lengthwise and mince the garlic.

3. Halve the chicken breasts and place them in a single layer in a large resealable plastic bag (or two smaller ones). With the chicken inside the bag, gently pound the chicken with a tenderizer or rolling pin to an even ¼-inch thickness.

4. To the bag with the chicken, add the flour, paprika, Italian seasoning, 1 teaspoon salt, and a few twists of black pepper. Seal the bag and shake it well until the chicken is evenly coated in the flour and spices.

5. In a large nonstick pan or well-seasoned cast-iron skillet over medium heat, melt 2 tablespoons of the butter.

6. Add the chicken in a single layer. Sear it on both sides until deep golden brown and 165°F in the thickest part, 4 to 6 minutes total. Work in batches if necessary, transferring the cooked pieces to a plate and adding some more butter or some cooking oil if the pan looks dry.

7. When you've cooked all the chicken, melt the remaining 2 tablespoons of butter.

CONTINUES →

8. Add the cherry tomatoes in a single layer. You want as many as possible to touch the bottom of the pan. Cook without stirring until the tomatoes start to sizzle and brown in spots, 5 to 7 minutes.

9. By now, the pasta water should be boiling. Add the pasta and cook according to package directions.

10. Add the garlic and balsamic vinegar to the tomatoes. Continue cooking, stirring often, until the tomatoes start to fall apart and lose their shape, 2 to 7 more minutes, depending on their freshness and juiciness. Scrape any browned bits from the bottom of the pan.

11. Return the chicken and any juices to the pan. Spoon the tomatoes and their liquid over the chicken for 1 or 2 minutes until the chicken warms back up.

12. Drain the pasta and transfer it to a large serving plate. Arrange the chicken over the pasta and spoon the tomatoes and sauce over the top. Top with the Parmesan cheese.

VARIATIONS

Feel free to skip the pasta and serve the chicken and sauce over a grain instead, such as couscous, farro, or quinoa.

To make it vegetarian, replace the chicken with thick slices of portobello mushrooms or use a cheese that won't lose its shape when seared, such as paneer or Halloumi.

Pork and Basil Dumplings

WITH CHILI CRISP TOMATOES

Summer flavors meet dumplings and hot chili oil in this mash-up of flavors that tastes even better than it sounds. The tomatoes turn tender and saucy, adding depth to the garlic and shallot chili crisp and making their flavors stretch further. Forming dumplings isn't fun if you're in a rush, so give yourself enough time to enjoy the process.

SERVES 4   PREP: 35 MINUTES   COOK: 20 MINUTES   TOTAL: 55 MINUTES

cutting board · knife · large mixing bowl · rimmed baking sheet · parchment · small bowl · large nonstick pan

---

1½ cups cherry or grape tomatoes

3 cloves garlic

1 shallot

20 leaves fresh basil, plus more for garnish

1 pound ground pork

1 tablespoon fish sauce

¼ teaspoon kosher salt

24 square or round dumpling or potsticker wrappers

¼ cup plus 1 tablespoon cooking oil

¼ cup water

½ teaspoon red pepper flakes

1. Halve the tomatoes lengthwise. Mince the garlic and shallot. Finely chop the basil.

2. In a large mixing bowl, combine the ground pork, one-third of the minced garlic, fish sauce, basil, and salt.

3. Line a baking sheet with parchment paper, fill a small bowl with water, and dampen a paper towel.

4. Fill 1 dumpling or potsticker wrapper with 1 tablespoon of the pork mixture. Dip your fingers in the bowl of water and run them around the edges of each wrapper. Gather the edges of the wrapper, pinch them closed tightly like a little bag, and press to flatten the bottom of the dumpling.

5. Place the finished dumplings on the prepared baking sheet and cover with the damp paper towel.

6. When you've made all the dumplings, place your largest lidded nonstick pan over medium heat and heat 1 tablespoon of the cooking oil. When the oil shimmers, add the dumplings in a single layer and cook without moving them until the bottoms turn golden brown, about 3 minutes. Work in batches if necessary.

7. Pour the ¼ cup water down the side of the pan and cover. Cook for 5 minutes. To test for doneness, remove 1 dumpling and slice it open to see if the filling has cooked.

CONTINUES →

8. Remove the lid and continue cooking, uncovered, until all the water evaporates.

9. Transfer the cooked dumplings to a serving platter or bowl, leaving space among them. Cover to keep them warm.

10. Return the pan to medium heat and add 3 tablespoons of oil, the remaining minced garlic, shallot, and red pepper flakes. Cook, stirring constantly, until the veggies lightly toast and become fragrant, about 3 minutes. Transfer to a small bowl.

11. Increase the heat to medium-high. Add the remaining 1 tablespoon of oil. Add the sliced tomatoes and cook until they burst, about 5 minutes. Stir the tomatoes into the chili oil.

12. Spoon the warm tomato chili oil evenly around and on the dumplings.

13. Garnish each dumpling with a few torn basil leaves and serve warm.

VARIATION

To make it vegetarian, mix it up. The protein in the filling matters less than the other components. A combination of mushrooms and tofu, chopped evenly in a food processor, works just as well as any ground meat.

Harissa Gazpacho

It often becomes too hot to use the stove at the exact moment that gardens and farmers' markets are overflowing with tomatoes. That's the time for gazpacho, which requires no heat and can use up pounds of peak-season tomatoes. I love to serve gazpacho as a starter instead of the main event while something more substantial cooks on the grill. In this version, smoky, spicy harissa adds an extra dimension to the rich, fresh flavors of the classic summer dish. Try serving it in small cocktail glasses, garnished with cherry tomatoes or cucumber slices.

SERVES 6   PREP: 20 MINUTES, PLUS CHILLING TIME   TOTAL: 4 HOURS 20 MINUTES
cutting board · knife · blender

---

2 slices white sandwich bread, No-Knead Focaccia (page 246), ciabatta, or baguette

2 pounds heirloom tomatoes

¾ teaspoon kosher salt

8 ounces seedless cucumbers

1 clove garlic

1 red or yellow bell pepper

¼ small red onion

¼ cup olive oil, plus extra for serving

2 tablespoons harissa paste

1 tablespoon Sherry or white wine vinegar

cherry tomatoes or extra cucumber slices for garnish (optional)

1. If the bread has a thick or dark crust, remove and discard it. Tear the bread roughly into 2-inch pieces and place them in a high-speed blender or food processor.

2. Roughly chop the tomatoes and combine them with the salt. Add the tomatoes to the blender or food processor.

3. Peel and roughly chop the cucumbers. Peel the garlic. Chop the bell pepper and onion into pieces that fit easily in your blender or food processor.

4. Add the cucumbers, bell pepper, onion, garlic, olive oil, harissa, and vinegar to the blender or food processor. Blend or process until very smooth. If necessary, add a small amount of water.

5. Refrigerate the gazpacho until ready to serve, at least 4 hours and up to 2 days.

6. Pour into small glasses, drizzle with olive oil, and garnish with cherry tomatoes or cucumber slices if desired.

NOTE: In concentrated form, harissa contains many ingredients already in the gazpacho, so if you don't have any harissa, you can make the soup without it. In that case, consider adding red pepper flakes or hot sauce for a little extra spice.

 TIP Different color tomatoes and peppers will give you different colors of gazpacho. Use yellow tomatoes and peppers for golden gazpacho or red tomatoes and peppers for a classic red version.

Green Beans

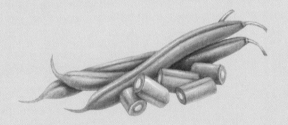

Green Bean Curry Fried Rice

Leftover rice is like money in the bank. You can use it to put dinner on the table in about 30 minutes. For this recipe, chop the green beans small so they cook fast and give good crunch. Green curry adds fresh, herby notes that go incredibly well here, but red curry paste works just fine, too.

SERVES 4   PREP: 10 MINUTES   COOK: 20 MINUTES   TOTAL: 30 MINUTES
cutting board • knife • small bowl • whisk • wok or nonstick pan • large mixing bowl

---

10 ounces green beans

1 large lime

8 strips bacon

3 tablespoons low-sodium soy sauce or tamari

1 tablespoon rice vinegar

1 to 3 tablespoons green curry paste

3 eggs

½ teaspoon kosher salt

2 tablespoons cooking oil

5 cups leftover or cooled jasmine rice

hot sauce for serving (optional)

1. Chop the green beans into ¼-inch pieces. Slice the lime into wedges. Roughly chop the bacon.

2. In a small bowl, whisk together the soy sauce, rice vinegar, and green curry paste. Add more or less green curry to taste.

3. In a small bowl, whisk the eggs with ¼ teaspoon of the salt.

4. In a wok or nonstick pan over medium heat, heat 1 tablespoon of the cooking oil, add the whisked eggs, and scramble gently until the eggs just cook through, 3 to 4 minutes. Transfer the eggs to a large mixing bowl. Cover to keep them warm.

5. Return the pan to the heat and add the chopped bacon. Cook, stirring often, until very crisp, 6 to 7 minutes. Transfer the bacon to a paper towel–lined plate to drain and cool. From the pan, drain all but a thin layer of bacon grease.

6. Increase the heat to medium-high. Add the green beans and stir to coat them in bacon grease. Spread them in a single layer and cook, without stirring, until they start popping and have browned on the bottom, 3 to 4 minutes.

7. Add the remaining ¼ teaspoon salt. Cook, stirring constantly, until fragrant, about 1 minute. Transfer the green beans to the bowl with the eggs and replace the cover.

8. Return the pan to the heat and add the remaining 1 tablespoon of oil. Add the rice, crumbling any large clumps.

9. Add the green curry sauce and stir gently to combine.

CONTINUES →

10. Spread the rice evenly in the pan and cook, undisturbed, until it browns and crisps, 3 to 4 minutes.

11. Gently stir the rice a few more times to heat it through.

12. Add the rice to the eggs and green beans and stir to combine.

13. Transfer to four individual serving bowls and crumble the bacon on each serving. Top with hot sauce if you'd like. Serve lime wedges on the side for squeezing over the rice.

VARIATION

To make it vegetarian, skip the bacon and stir roasted cashews into the finished dish.

Green Beans
WITH PICKLED PEPPER VINAIGRETTE

In this warm-weather side dish, sweet-tart dressing balances the earthiness of the green beans. Dunking the green beans in ice water stops the cooking process and cools them, but you can skip that step and serve them warm, too. If your grocery store has an olive bar, look for Peppadew® there and buy exactly the amount you need. Otherwise, you should be able to find them shelved near the jars of roasted red peppers.

SERVES 4 TO 6   PREP: 10 MINUTES   COOK: 10 MINUTES   TOTAL: 20 MINUTES
saucepan • cutting board • knife • small bowl or jar • mixing bowls • colander

---

¼ teaspoon salt, plus more for the pot

1 pound green beans

1 shallot

4 sweet pickled peppers, such as Peppadew

1 tablespoon pickle liquid from the peppers

1 tablespoon red wine vinegar

1 teaspoon Dijon mustard

⅓ cup olive oil

1. Fill a large saucepan half full with water, place it over medium-high heat, and salt it generously, about 1 teaspoon. Don't worry about measuring but also don't skimp. Bring the water to a boil.

2. Meanwhile, stem the green beans and dice the shallot. Dice the pickled peppers, reserving the liquid.

3. In a small bowl or jar, whisk or shake together the peppers, pepper liquid, red wine vinegar, mustard, and ¼ teaspoon salt. If using a bowl, add the olive oil while whisking.

4. Fill a medium mixing bowl with 2 cups of ice and then half full of cold water.

5. When the water boils, add the green beans and cook until bright green and tender but still crisp, 3 minutes for French green beans (haricots verts) and up to 6 minutes for thicker green beans.

6. Transfer the green beans to the ice water bath and chill them for at least 5 minutes.

7. Drain the green beans and pat them dry.

8. In a large mixing bowl, add the green beans and the vinaigrette. Stir to coat evenly.

9. Spread the green beans on a serving platter, spooning the vinaigrette from the bottom of the mixing bowl onto them.

Peanut Noodles

WITH GREEN BEANS

Come for the veggies but stay for the sauce. Saucy noodles please a crowd, and the green beans and chopped peanuts both provide great crunch.

SERVES 4   PREP: 20 MINUTES   COOK: 12 MINUTES   TOTAL: 32 MINUTES
stockpot · cutting board · knife · small bowl or jar · mixing bowl

---

kosher salt for the pot

10 ounces green beans, fresh or frozen

½ cup roasted unsalted peanuts

1 pound dry spaghetti or udon noodles

1 batch Peanut Sauce (page 244)

sesame seeds for garnish

VARIATION

To make it a main dish, top the noodles with Pan-Fried Tofu (page 5) or diced chicken.

1. Fill a stockpot half full with water, place it over medium-high heat, and salt it generously, about 1 tablespoon. Don't worry about measuring but also don't skimp. Bring the water to a boil.

2. If using fresh green beans, stem them and chop them into 1-inch pieces. If using frozen, defrost them.

3. Roughly chop the peanuts.

4. Cook the noodles according to package directions.

5. When 6 minutes of cooking time for the noodles remain, add regular green beans to the boiling water. If using French green beans (haricots verts), add with 3 minutes left. If using frozen, add with 1 minute left.

6. Drain the noodles and green beans well, transfer them to a serving bowl, and add the Peanut Sauce. Gently stir to coat and thicken.

7. Top with peanuts or sesame seeds if using and serve warm.

DOUBLE UP!

Make a double batch of Peanut Sauce (page 244) and use it to make Asparagus Summer Rolls (page 185).

Green Bean and Potato Salad

No one will overlook this potato salad at your next gathering. With fresh green beans and a super-tangy dressing, it's a salad that will have everyone going back for more. It also has great versatility. Serve it warm in cool weather or chilled in hot weather.

SERVES 4 TO 6 PREP: 20 MINUTES COOK: 20 MINUTES TOTAL: 40 MINUTES
stockpot • cutting board • knife • large skillet • large mixing bowl

kosher salt for the pot

8 ounces green beans (see Note)

1½ pounds baby red potatoes

¼ bunch fresh chives

1 small red onion

1 tablespoon cooking oil

6 ounces diced pancetta

⅓ cup olive oil

¼ cup apple cider vinegar

1½ tablespoons stone-ground Dijon mustard

black pepper

VARIATIONS

To make it vegetarian, skip the pancetta.

To make it a main dish, add a can of drained and rinsed white beans to the finished dish.

1. Fill a stockpot half full with water, place it over medium-high heat, and salt it generously, about 1 tablespoon. Don't worry about measuring but also don't skimp. Bring the water to a boil.

2. Stem the green beans and chop them into 3-inch lengths. Halve or quarter the potatoes, depending on size. You want 2-inch-thick wedges.

3. Chop the chives and dice the onion.

4. When the water boils, add the potatoes and cook until a fork easily pierces them, about 15 minutes.

5. When 6 minutes of cooking time for the potatoes remain, add regular green beans to the boiling water. If using French green beans (haricots verts), add with 3 minutes left. Drain the cooked veggies well.

6. Meanwhile, in a large skillet over medium heat, heat the cooking oil and add the pancetta and onions. Cook, stirring often, until the pancetta becomes crisp and golden, 5 to 7 minutes. Remove the pan from the heat and whisk in the olive oil, apple cider vinegar, and mustard.

7. In a large mixing bowl, combine the potatoes, green beans, and chives with the dressing. Top with black pepper. Serve warm, at room temperature, or chilled.

NOTE: You can use any green beans in this recipe, but thinner French green beans (haricots verts) cook faster, and their smaller shape means more of them in every bite.

 TIP Look for diced pancetta in the deli section of your grocery store. If they don't have it, ask the deli clerk for help.

Green Bean and Ginger Wraps
WITH CHICKEN

Pickled ginger, the kind served with sushi, gives these wraps a tart, spicy kick. Look for it in the Asian or international aisle of your grocery store. You can skip searing the wraps, but that final step helps them stay together and gives them a nice, crunchy texture.

SERVES 4   PREP: 20 MINUTES   COOK: 40 MINUTES   TOTAL: 1 HOUR

medium saucepan or rice cooker • cutting board • knife • medium mixing bowl • small bowl • colander • large nonstick pan or skillet

---

1 cup uncooked white or brown rice

kosher salt for the pot

10 ounces fresh green beans

1½ cups shredded cooked chicken

4 burrito-size flour tortillas

1 batch Gochujang Yogurt Sauce (page 240)

¼ cup pickled ginger

2 teaspoons cooking oil

1. On the stovetop or using a rice cooker, cook the rice according to package directions.

2. Fill a large saucepan half full with water, place it over medium-high heat, and add about 1 teaspoon of salt. Don't worry about measuring but also don't skimp. Bring the water to a boil.

3. Stem the green beans.

4. Fill a medium mixing bowl with 2 cups of ice and then half full of cold water.

5. When the water boils, add the green beans and cook them until bright green and tender but still crisp, 3 minutes for French green beans (haricots verts) and up to 6 minutes for thicker green beans.

6. Transfer the green beans to the ice water to chill them for 5 minutes.

7. Drain the green beans and pat them dry.

8. If cold, reheat the chicken in the microwave until warm but not hot, on high for about 1 minute.

9. Assemble the wraps by filling each tortilla with ½ cup of rice, 1 tablespoon of Gochujang Yogurt Sauce, a layer of green beans, 1 tablespoon of the pickled ginger, and a layer of chicken. Top with another 1 tablespoon of Gochujang Yogurt Sauce. Roll up each wrap, tucking in the sides like a burrito.

CONTINUES →

10. In your largest nonstick pan or skillet over medium heat, heat the cooking oil and add the wraps, seam-sides down. It's OK if they touch. Cook until crispy, then turn them and sear on the opposite side, about 6 minutes total. Press the wraps gently as they cook. In this step, you're not necessarily trying to heat the filling but to crisp the tortillas.

11. Serve with extra Gochujang Yogurt Sauce for dipping.

NOTE: You can assemble the wraps ahead of time and refrigerate them, tightly wrapped in foil, for up to 2 days. Warm them up, still in foil, in a 425°F oven for 15 to 20 minutes.

DOUBLE UP!

Make a double batch of Gochujang Yogurt Sauce (page 240) and use the sauce to make No-Roll Sushi Bowls (page 143), Green Bean and Ginger Wraps with Chicken (page 172), Banh Mi Bowls with Quick-Pickled Carrots (page 25), and/or Sweet Potatoes, Broccoli, and Gochujang Chicken (page 61).

VARIATION

To make it vegetarian, use 1½ cups of shelled edamame instead of the chicken. Many grocery stores carry shelled edamame in the freezer section. Just defrost it before adding it to the wraps.

Asparagus

ASPARAGUS ORZO WITH
GOAT CHEESE AND LEMON   176

ASPARAGUS FRITTATAS
WITH GRUYÈRE AND HAM   179

PICNIC SANDWICHES
WITH BASIL DIJONNAISE   180

GREEN GODDESS GRAIN BOWLS
WITH ASPARAGUS AND CHICKEN   183

ASPARAGUS SUMMER ROLLS
WITH PEANUT SAUCE   185

Asparagus Orzo
WITH GOAT CHEESE AND LEMON

The best part about this springy pasta dish isn't the fresh crunch of the asparagus, the brightness of the lemon, or the creaminess of the goat cheese. It's that you can make it in just one pan.

SERVES 4   PREP: 10 MINUTES   COOK: 20 MINUTES   TOTAL: 30 MINUTES
cutting board • knife • small bowl • large lidded sauté pan

---

1 bunch asparagus (1 pound)

2 cloves garlic

1 lemon

¼ cup pine nuts

3 tablespoons unsalted butter

3 cups low-sodium vegetable stock

1½ cups dry orzo pasta

½ teaspoon kosher salt

4 ounces goat cheese

1. Stem the asparagus at the point where the stalks turn tough and woody. Chop the asparagus into 1-inch pieces. Mince the garlic. Into a small bowl, zest the lemon and juice it.

2. In a large lidded sauté pan over medium heat, add the pine nuts and dry-cook them until golden brown and toasted, 3 to 4 minutes. Shake the pan often to prevent scorching. Transfer the pine nuts to a plate to cool.

3. Return the pan to the heat and melt the butter. Add the garlic and orzo and sauté until the garlic is fragrant and the orzo is coated in butter, about 1 minute.

4. Add the stock and, when it comes to a simmer, add the asparagus and salt. Cover the saucepan and reduce the heat to medium-low to maintain a low simmer. Cook the orzo until tender, 10 to 12 minutes. Remove the lid a few times to stir, focusing on the bottom of the pan, where the pasta likely will stick.

5. Remove the pan from the heat and add the lemon zest and juice and half of the goat cheese. Stir 20 times to thicken the mixture and make it creamy. It may still seem a bit liquidy, but it will continue to thicken as it sits.

6. Crumble the remaining goat cheese on the orzo, top it with the pine nuts, and serve warm.

> **VARIATION**
> To make it a main dish, top it with seared fish, shrimp, or tofu.

Asparagus Frittatas

WITH GRUYÈRE AND HAM

These frittatas work great on toast, and they fit perfectly inside a toasted English muffin for breakfast sliders. They also make an easy lunch with a salad on the side. Eggs tend to stick, so be sure to oil or spray your muffin pan generously, or use muffin liners for even easier cleanup.

MAKES 12 FRITTATAS   PREP: 20 MINUTES   COOK: 18 MINUTES   TOTAL: 38 MINUTES
cutting board · knife · medium skillet · medium bowl · muffin pan

1 bunch asparagus (1 pound)

2 ounces deli ham

4 ounces Gruyère cheese

1 tablespoon cooking oil

½ teaspoon kosher salt

8 large eggs

2 tablespoons milk, any type

black pepper

nonstick cooking spray or cooking oil

1. In the oven, place a rack in the middle position and preheat it to 350°F.

2. Stem the asparagus at the point where the stalks turn tough and woody. Chop the asparagus into ¼-inch pieces. Dice the ham and grate the cheese.

3. In a medium skillet over medium heat, heat the cooking oil and add the asparagus and ¼ teaspoon of the salt. Sauté until the asparagus turns bright green and tender, 4 to 8 minutes, depending on thickness.

4. In a medium bowl, whisk the eggs with the milk, the remaining ¼ teaspoon salt, and black pepper.

5. Generously spray a nonstick muffin pan with nonstick cooking spray or brush it with cooking oil. Fill each cavity halfway with the eggs. Top with asparagus, Gruyère, and ham. Add the remaining eggs to each cavity, just below the top.

6. Bake until the eggs set, 14 to 17 minutes.

7. Serve immediately or refrigerate for up to 3 days.

> **VARIATION**
> To make it vegetarian, skip the ham. Add 2 tablespoons of fresh minced chives or 1 tablespoon of fresh chopped dill for an added hit of flavor.

Picnic Sandwiches

WITH BASIL DIJONNAISE

Whether you're having a picnic or joining one, or just making lunch at home, this sandwich feels like a walk in the park. Enjoy it with your favorite potato chips and a fizzy drink.

SERVES 4 PREP: 30 MINUTES COOK: 10 MINUTES TOTAL: 40 MINUTES

cutting board • knife • immersion or countertop blender (optional) • small bowl • rimmed baking sheet

---

1 loaf crusty soft bread, such as baguette, ciabatta, or focaccia

1 bunch asparagus (1 pound)

1 tablespoon olive oil

½ teaspoon kosher salt

10 large leaves fresh basil

½ cup mayonnaise

2 teaspoons lemon juice

2 teaspoons Dijon mustard

4 ounces Brie cheese

6 ounces thinly sliced prosciutto

2 cups baby arugula or baby spinach

VARIATION

To make it vegetarian, make a batch of Red Lentil Bites (page 13), halve or quarter them, and layer them in the sandwiches. You'll need about 10 balls. They'll crumble slightly as you press the sandwich, but they taste great with the other flavors in the sandwich.

1. If softening the bread, preheat the oven to 425°F. See step 5.

2. Stem the asparagus at the point where the stalks turn tough and woody. Spread the asparagus on a rimmed baking sheet. Drizzle with olive oil and sprinkle with salt. Roast until the asparagus becomes tender, 10 minutes for thin spears and up to 20 minutes for very thick spears. Shake the pan halfway through cooking.

3. Meanwhile, make the Dijonnaise. If you have an immersion blender or small countertop blender, leave the basil leaves whole. If mixing the sauce by hand, mince the basil.

4. In a small bowl, whisk together the mayonnaise, basil, lemon juice, and mustard or blend if using a blender.

5. Slice the bread lengthwise horizontally. If it isn't super fresh, heat it, cut sides up, in the oven for 4 minutes to soften it slightly.

6. Spread both sides of the bread with basil Dijonnaise.

7. Cut the Brie, rind on, into thin slices. If the asparagus stalks are too thick to bite easily, halve them lengthwise. Fill the bread with Brie, asparagus, prosciutto, and baby arugula.

8. Gently press the completed sandwich and slice it into four equal pieces.

9. Serve immediately or wrap tightly, keep cool, and serve within a couple of hours.

 TIP If you want to make the components in advance, roast the asparagus and make the Dijonnaise up to 3 days ahead. Leftover Dijonnaise will keep in the fridge for up to 3 days. It makes a great dip for vegetables or a spread for burgers and other sandwiches.

Green Goddess Grain Bowls

WITH ASPARAGUS AND CHICKEN

Green Goddess Sauce (page 245) does double duty in these colorful grain bowls. Separate the sauce into two portions, using one as a quick marinade that yields the most tender chicken and the rest for generous drizzling.

SERVES 4   PREP: 40 MINUTES   COOK: 20 MINUTES   TOTAL: 1 HOUR

saucepan • cutting board • knife • small bowl • 16-ounce jar • mixing bowls • large nonstick pan or cast-iron skillet

---

¾ teaspoon kosher salt, plus more for the pot

2 cups uncooked pearled farro (see Variations)

1 batch Green Goddess Sauce (page 245)

½ cup whole almonds

1 bunch asparagus (1 pound)

1 pound boneless, skinless chicken breast

black pepper

2 tablespoons cooking oil

1 batch Pickled Red Onions (page 245)

1. Fill a stockpot half full with water, place it over medium-high heat, and salt it generously, about 1 tablespoon. Don't worry about measuring but also don't skimp. Bring the water to a boil.

2. By now, the water should be boiling. Rinse the farro well under cool water, then add it to the boiling water. Reduce the heat to medium-low to maintain a gentle simmer and cook, stirring occasionally, until the farro has an al dente bite and chewy texture, 15 to 20 minutes.

3. Roughly chop the almonds. Stem the asparagus at the point where the stalks turn tough and woody. If the spears don't fit easily in a sauté pan, cut them into smaller pieces.

4. Halve the chicken lengthwise.

5. In a medium mixing bowl, combine the chicken, ¼ cup of the Green Goddess Sauce, ½ teaspoon of salt, and a few twists of black pepper, coating evenly. Reserve the rest of the Green Goddess Sauce for topping.

6. In your largest nonstick pan or well-seasoned cast-iron skillet over medium heat, add 1 tablespoon of cooking oil, the asparagus, and ¼ teaspoon salt. Cook, rotating the asparagus occasionally, until tender, 4 to 8 minutes, depending on the spears' thickness. Transfer the cooked asparagus to a bowl.

CONTINUES →

7. Reduce the heat to medium-low and add the remaining 1 tablespoon of the olive oil and the chicken in a single layer. Cook the chicken on both sides until golden brown and cooked through, 4 to 8 minutes total.

8. Transfer the chicken to a cutting board, and let it rest for 5 minutes.

9. At this point, the farro should be done cooking. Drain and rinse it to stop the cooking process.

10. After the chicken has rested, thinly slice it. Assemble the bowls in this order: farro, asparagus, chicken, Pickled Red Onions, almonds, and the remaining Green Goddess Sauce.

DOUBLE UP!

Make a double batch of Green Goddess Sauce (page 245) and use it for Zucchini and Corn Tostadas (page 111) or BLAT Salad (page 152).

TIP This recipe uses Pickled Red Onions (page 245), but you may not need all of them for these grain bowls. If you have any left over, use them to make Sweet Potato Cobb Salad (page 55).

VARIATIONS

Instead of farro, use your grain of choice, such as quinoa or brown rice.

To make it vegetarian, skip the chicken and marinade and top the bowls with Roasted Chickpeas (page 6).

Asparagus Summer Rolls

WITH PEANUT SAUCE

Soba noodles traditionally don't go in summer rolls, but their flavor pairs incredibly well with the earthiness of asparagus. Making 16 summer rolls yourself can become a time-consuming process, so turn it into a group activity. Set out all the ingredients and let everyone make their own rolls as they eat. Have extra rice paper wrappers on hand in case a few break while everyone gets the hang of it.

MAKES 16 ROLLS   PREP: 50 MINUTES   COOK: 10 MINUTES   TOTAL: 1 HOUR
saucepan • cutting board • knife • small bowl or jar • medium mixing bowl, shallow bowl

---

kosher salt for the pot

1 bunch asparagus (1 pound)

16 rice paper wrappers, plus a few extra

6 ounces dry soba noodles

16 small leaves mild lettuce, such as butter or Boston

½ cup loosely packed fresh basil, cilantro, and/or mint leaves

1 batch Peanut Sauce (page 244)

1. Fill a large saucepan half full with water, place it over medium-high heat, and add about 1 teaspoon of salt. Don't worry about measuring but also don't skimp. Bring the water to a boil.

2. While you wait for the water to boil, stem the asparagus at the point where the stalks turn tough and woody. If the stemmed spears are longer than the diameter of the rice paper wrappers, halve the stalks crosswise to shorten them.

3. Fill a medium mixing bowl with 2 cups of ice and then half full of cold water.

4. When the water in the saucepan boils, add the asparagus and cook until the spears turn bright green and tender, 2 to 5 minutes, depending on the stalks' thickness.

5. Use heatproof tongs to remove the asparagus from the boiling water and transfer it to the ice water for 5 minutes. Leave the pan of water boiling on the stove.

6. While the asparagus cools, add the soba noodles to the boiling water and cook according to package directions.

7. Transfer the soba noodles to the ice water with the asparagus so they also cool quickly. Drain the asparagus and noodles well.

8. Set out the asparagus, soba noodles, lettuce, herbs, and rice paper wrappers.

CONTINUES →

9. If you're assembling the rolls yourself, line a baking sheet with wax or parchment paper.

10. Fill a shallow bowl with warm water that doesn't feel too hot to touch. Hot water from the tap works great for this step.

11. Soak a rice paper wrapper in the warm water until it just begins to soften, 4 to 8 seconds. Drain excess water and transfer the wrapper to a flat surface.

12. Fill the wrapper with a lettuce leaf, fresh herbs, soba noodles, and asparagus. Don't overfill. Fold the bottom edge over the filling, fold the sides to enclose it, and then completely roll it up.

13. If you're assembling the rolls yourself, transfer them to the prepared baking sheet as you go, keeping them loosely covered with a damp paper towel to keep them moist.

14. Serve immediately with the Peanut Sauce.

DOUBLE UP!

Make a double batch of Peanut Sauce (page 244) and use it to make Peanut Noodles with Green Beans (page 168).

Brussels Sprouts

ORECCHIETTE WITH CARAMELIZED BRUSSELS
SPROUTS AND BACON   189

SHREDDED BRUSSELS SPROUTS SALAD WITH
POPPYSEED DRESSING   193

TURKEY AND CHEESE PRETZEL MELTS WITH
BRUSSELS SPROUTS SLAW   194

CITRUS SHRIMP AND BRUSSELS SPROUTS
WITH CRISPY RICE   197

PITA CRUNCH SALAD
WITH ROASTED BRUSSELS SPROUTS   200

Orecchiette

WITH CARAMELIZED BRUSSELS SPROUTS AND BACON

When mac and cheese grows up, the dish looks like this: creamy pasta, tender veggies, and crunchy bacon in every bite.

SERVES 4   PREP: 10 MINUTES   COOK: 30 MINUTES   TOTAL: 40 MINUTES
stockpot · cutting board · knife · large sauté pan · box grater

kosher salt for the pot

1 pound shredded Brussels sprouts

3 cloves garlic

8 slices bacon

1 pound uncooked orecchiette pasta

3 ounces Parmesan cheese

¼ cup heavy cream

black pepper

1. Fill a stockpot half full with water, place it over medium-high heat, and salt it generously, about 1 tablespoon. Don't worry about measuring but also don't skimp. Bring the water to a boil.

2. Sort through the Brussels sprouts and discard any tough stems. Mince the garlic.

3. In your largest sauté pan over medium-low heat, add the bacon and cook on both sides until crisp, 6 to 8 minutes total. Transfer the cooked bacon to a paper towel–lined plate to drain and cool. Drain all but a thin layer of bacon grease from the pan.

4. By now, the water should be boiling. Add the pasta and cook according to package directions.

5. Return the sauté pan with the bacon grease to medium heat. Add the Brussels sprouts and garlic and cook, without stirring, until the sprouts soften slightly and start to caramelize where they are touching the pan, 2 to 3 minutes. Stir gently and continue cooking until the sprouts are just tender but still have some crunch, 1 to 4 minutes (depending on how thickly shredded they are). Remove from the heat.

6. Grate the Parmesan cheese. You should have about 1 cup.

CONTINUES →

7. When the pasta finishes cooking, reserve ½ cup of pasta water. Drain the pasta and add it to the pan with the Brussels sprouts. Stir in the Parmesan cheese and cream. A little at a time, add the pasta water until the sauce coats the pasta. You may not need all the pasta water.

8. Taste the pasta and season with some salt, if needed. Often the seasoned pasta water, the bacon grease, and the Parmesan add enough salty flavor to the dish, but taste and adjust as needed.

9. Divide the pasta among the serving bowls. Top with a few twists of black pepper and crumble the bacon on it.

TIP Look for shredded Brussels sprouts in the produce section of your grocery store. If you can't find them, buy 1 pound of Brussels sprouts, stem them, and use the shredding disk of a food processor to shred them.

Shredded Brussels Sprouts Salad
WITH POPPYSEED DRESSING

Many of us shudder at the memory of the boiled, bitter Brussels sprouts that our parents made, but these little cabbages have come a long way since then. In the 1990s, a Dutch scientist identified the molecules that make Brussels sprouts taste bitter, and since then growers have created less bitter varieties for a naturally sweeter sprout. If you're unsure about eating them raw, the sweet, subtle zing of poppyseed dressing might win you over.

SERVES 4   PREP: 20 MINUTES   TOTAL: 20 MINUTES
cutting board • knife • small bowl or jar • whisk • large mixing bowl • vegetable peeler or box grater

1 pound shredded Brussels sprouts

1 shallot

3 tablespoons white vinegar

1½ tablespoons honey

2 teaspoons poppy seeds

1 teaspoon Dijon mustard

¼ teaspoon kosher salt

⅓ cup olive oil

½ cup dried cranberries

¼ cup roasted, unsalted sunflower seeds

2 ounces Parmesan cheese

1. Sort through the Brussels sprouts and discard any tough stems. Mince the shallot.

2. In a small bowl or jar, whisk or shake together the shallot, vinegar, honey, poppy seeds, mustard, and salt. If using a bowl, slowly add the olive oil while whisking. If using a jar, add the olive oil and shake again until smooth.

3. In a large mixing bowl, combine the Brussels sprouts, cranberries, and sunflower seeds. Add the dressing, more or less to your liking, and stir to combine and coat evenly.

4. Use a vegetable peeler or box grater to grate the cheese on the salad. Serve immediately.

VARIATION

To make it a main dish, top the slaw with Pan-Fried Tofu (page 5) or seared salmon or steak.

TIP Look for shredded Brussels sprouts in the produce section of your grocery store. If you can't find them, buy 1 pound of Brussels sprouts, stem them, and use the shredding disk of a food processor to shred them.

Turkey and Cheese Pretzel Melts

WITH BRUSSELS SPROUTS SLAW

Do you need a recipe for a turkey and cheese sandwich? Probably not. Will this tangy, crisp Brussels sprouts slaw improve your turkey and cheese sandwich immensely? Yes.

SERVES 4   PREP: 20 MINUTES   COOK: 10 MINUTES   TOTAL: 30 MINUTES
large mixing bowl • rimmed baking sheet

10 ounces shredded Brussels sprouts

¼ cup mayonnaise

2 tablespoons whole-grain mustard

4 pretzel sandwich rolls or other hearty sandwich roll

12 ounces sliced deli turkey

4 slices provolone or Swiss cheese

3 tablespoons apple cider vinegar

2 tablespoons olive oil

½ teaspoon kosher salt

½ teaspoon honey

1. If your oven doesn't have a dedicated broiler, use the main compartment. Arrange a rack about 8 inches below the heat source and turn on the heat. If you have a broiler and it has more than one setting, use the low one.

2. Sort through the Brussels sprouts and discard any tough stems.

3. In a large mixing bowl, whisk together the mayonnaise and mustard.

4. On an unlined rimmed baking sheet, place the pretzel rolls, cut sides up. Brush the rolls lightly with the mayo-mustard. Don't use it all.

5. Broil the rolls until they turn golden brown, 3 to 6 minutes. Broiler temperatures can vary widely, so watch closely to avoid burning.

6. Set the tops of the toasted rolls aside and layer the bottom halves with turkey and cheese. Return the bottom halves to the broiler until the cheese melts and bubbles, 3 to 6 more minutes.

7. Meanwhile, whisk the vinegar, olive oil, salt, and honey into the remaining mayo-mustard dressing.

CONTINUES →

8. Add the shredded Brussels sprouts and stir well, coating evenly.

9. Top the turkey and cheese with a dollop of slaw and the tops of the toasted rolls and serve warm.

Look for shredded Brussels sprouts in the produce section of your grocery store. If you can't find them, buy 1 pound of Brussels sprouts, stem them, and use the shredding disk of a food processor to shred them.

VARIATION

To make it vegetarian, use 4 fried eggs instead of the turkey.

Citrus Shrimp and Brussels Sprouts
WITH CRISPY RICE

The sticky sauce in this stir-fry takes inspiration from orange chicken, although it's not quite as sweet as most versions of that dish. The Fresno chile peppers give it a good amount of spice, but feel free to adjust and use more or less if you'd prefer. This recipe works best with shrimp and Brussels sprouts of roughly equal size, which makes it easy to scoop both with the citrusy sauce and crunchy rice. Like fried rice, crispy rice makes great use of leftovers, so the next time you make rice, make extra!

SERVES 4 PREP: 20 MINUTES COOK: 20 MINUTES TOTAL: 40 MINUTES
cutting board · knife · small mixing bowl · large nonstick pan · hard spatula · wok or skillet

---

1 pound Brussels sprouts

2 cloves garlic

1-inch piece fresh ginger, peeled

2 Fresno chile peppers, more or less depending on your spice preference

1 cup pulp-free orange juice

3 tablespoons packed light brown sugar

¼ cup cooking oil

4 cups leftover or cooled long-grain white rice

½ teaspoon kosher salt

1 pound small peeled and deveined shrimp (50 to 60 per pound)

3 tablespoons low-sodium soy sauce

2 teaspoons cornstarch

20 small leaves fresh basil

1. Stem the Brussels sprouts and, if using large ones, halve or quarter them. Peel and thinly slice the garlic. Grate the ginger. Thinly slice the chiles.

2. In a small bowl, whisk together the orange juice, brown sugar, ginger, and garlic.

3. In a large nonstick pan over medium-low heat, add 2 tablespoons of the cooking oil and swirl the pan to coat it evenly. With a hard spatula, flatten the rice into the bottom and about 1 inch up the sides of the pan. Cook, without disturbing, until the rice crisps and becomes golden on the bottom, 8 to 10 minutes. Use a small spoon to lift portions of the rice to check that the crust is forming and that the rice isn't burning.

4. Meanwhile, in a wok or skillet over medium heat, add the remaining 2 tablespoons of cooking oil. When the oil is hot, add the Brussels sprouts in a single layer, cut sides down. Cook, undisturbed, until the sprouts turn a deep golden brown on the bottom, 5 to 6 minutes.

5. Add the salt and Fresno chiles. Cook, stirring, for 1 minute.

6. Add the shrimp to the Brussels sprouts and stir gently to combine.

CONTINUES →

7. Pour the orange juice mixture over the shrimp and Brussels sprouts. When the cooking liquid simmers, whisk together the soy sauce and cornstarch. Pour it into the skillet, stirring to combine.

8. Simmer, stirring occasionally, until the sauce reduces, the shrimp cook through, and the Brussels sprouts become tender, 4 to 5 more minutes.

9. With a wooden spoon or hard spatula, gently break the crispy rice into large pieces. Divide the rice among serving bowls. Flip some pieces over so you have plenty of crispy bits on top.

10. Stir the basil leaves into the Brussels sprouts and shrimp just until they wilt. Spoon the stir-fry over the crispy rice and serve warm.

VARIATION

To make it vegetarian, use a can of drained and rinsed chickpeas in place of the shrimp.

 TIP If you have leftover orange juice mixture, use it in Citrus, Carrot, and Chickpea Couscous (page 21).

Pita Crunch Salad

WITH ROASTED BRUSSELS SPROUTS

Packed salads taste great because they have so many delicious things happening all at the same time. Spiced crispy pita comes from fattoush salad, popular in countries on the eastern Mediterranean. Just like that salad, which inspired this dish, freshly toasted pita added right before serving helps it retain some crunch when it reaches your mouth.

SERVES 4 TO 6   PREP: 25 MINUTES   COOK: 25 MINUTES   TOTAL: 50 MINUTES
cutting board • knife • large mixing bowl • 2 rimmed baking sheets • parchment paper • small bowl

1 pound Brussels sprouts

3 pita rounds

½ cup olive oil

1½ teaspoons kosher salt

1 teaspoon dried thyme

1 teaspoon ground coriander

1 teaspoon smoked paprika

¼ cup apple cider vinegar

3 tablespoons tahini

2 teaspoons maple syrup

8 ounces mixed greens

½ cup pomegranate arils

3 ounces feta cheese

1. In the oven, arrange a rack in the lower position and another in the upper position. Preheat it to 425°F.

2. Stem the Brussels sprouts and, if using large ones, halve or quarter them. Save any leaves that fall off and roast them with the sprouts. They'll add extra-crispy crunch to the finished dish.

3. Gently separate the pita rounds to create 6 circles. Cut each circle into 2-inch squares. Don't worry if they're not all the same size. Some variation is good.

4. In a large mixing bowl, combine the Brussels sprouts, 2 tablespoons of the olive oil, and ½ teaspoon of the salt.

5. Spread the seasoned Brussels sprouts on an unlined rimmed baking sheet and roast on the upper rack until tender and golden, 20 to 25 minutes, stirring halfway through cooking.

6. Meanwhile, in the large mixing bowl you used for the Brussels sprouts, whisk together 2 tablespoons of the olive oil, the thyme, coriander, smoked paprika, and ½ teaspoon of salt.

7. Add the pita squares to the spice mixture and gently stir to coat them evenly, spooning the olive oil from the bottom of the bowl.

8. Line a second rimmed baking sheet with parchment paper. Spread the seasoned pita squares on it, keeping the mixing bowl nearby.

9. Bake the pita squares on the lower rack until crisp and a deep golden brown, 10 to 15 minutes, depending on the freshness of the pita. Fresher pita will need a little more time. Gently stir halfway through cooking.

10. In a small bowl, whisk together the vinegar, tahini, maple syrup, and the remaining ½ teaspoon salt. While whisking, add the remaining ¼ cup of olive oil.

11. In the large mixing bowl, combine the mixed greens, Brussels sprouts, three-quarters of the pita chips, and half of the dressing, coating evenly.

12. Top with the pomegranate arils. Crumble the feta and the remaining pita chips on top. Serve with the remaining dressing on the side.

NOTE: Pomegranate arils contain the seed plus the juice packet around it. Now you know! To save time, look for packaged arils or, if you can't find any, substitute dried cranberries.

DOUBLE UP!

Make a double batch of Maple Tahini Dressing (page 241) and use it in Roasted Carrot and Orzo Salad (page 15).

Kale and Spinach

Spinach Pesto Pasta

You can make pesto with more than just basil. This version uses baby spinach, which gives you a great way to use those greens. The resulting pesto tastes just as green and fresh as the basil version but with a milder flavor that lets the Parmesan cheese, garlic, and lemon shine. If you have baby spinach in your fridge with no plans to use it, do your future self a favor. Spend 20 minutes to whip up this dish. Use the pesto, tossed with pasta—as in this recipe—or anywhere that you'd use basil pesto. It freezes well, too.

SERVES 4 TO 6   PREP: 10 MINUTES   COOK: 10 MINUTES   TOTAL: 20 MINUTES
stockpot · cutting board · knife

---

kosher salt for the pot

2-inch chunk Parmesan cheese, plus more for serving

1 large lemon

5 ounces baby spinach

¼ cup slivered almonds

1 clove garlic

¼ teaspoon red pepper flakes

2 teaspoons balsamic vinegar

½ teaspoon kosher salt

⅓ cup olive oil

1 pound pasta of choice

black pepper

1. Fill a stockpot half full with water, place it over high heat, and salt it generously, about 1 tablespoon. Don't worry about measuring but also don't skimp. Bring the water to a boil.

2. While you wait for the water to boil, chop the Parmesan cheese into smaller chunks.

3. Juice the lemon for 1½ tablespoons of fresh juice.

4. In a food processor, add the cheese, baby spinach, slivered almonds, garlic, red pepper flakes, balsamic vinegar, salt, and lemon juice. Pulse a few times to break everything up. With the processor running, slowly add the olive oil.

5. Taste the pesto and add salt if necessary.

6. Boil the pasta according to package directions. Drain well.

7. Stir the pesto into the pasta. Top with grated Parmesan cheese and a few twists of black pepper. Serve warm.

> **VARIATIONS**
>
> Baby arugula also works well and creates a pesto with a more peppery bite. Use any combination of greens that you like.

Pearl Couscous Salad

WITH SUN-DRIED TOMATO VINAIGRETTE

I tested many pearl couscous salads for this book. Without exception, this version always won. Chopping the kale extra fine makes this salad feel a little virtuous. But the "secret" is to make the vinaigrette using the oil from a jar of sun-dried tomatoes, infusing the entire dish with savory tomato flavor.

SERVES 4 TO 6   PREP: 15 MINUTES   COOK: 10 MINUTES   TOTAL: 25 MINUTES
stockpot • large serving bowl • cutting board • knife • mixing bowl

---

kosher salt for the pot

2 large leaves curly kale

2 cups dry pearl couscous

1 batch Sun-Dried Tomato Vinaigrette (page 242)

4 ounces feta cheese

¼ cup toasted pine nuts or slivered almonds (optional)

VARIATION

To make it a main dish, stir in 1 can of drained and rinsed white beans or top with seared chicken, fish, or roasted portobello mushrooms.

1. Fill a large stockpot half full with water, place it over high heat, and salt it generously, about 1 tablespoon. Don't worry about measuring but don't skimp. Bring the water to a boil.

2. While you wait for the water to boil, stem the kale leaves, discard the stems, and finely chop the leaves.

3. When the water is boiling, stir in the pearl couscous and cook according to package directions. Drain and rinse with cool water.

4. Put the couscous in a large serving bowl. Add the Sun-Dried Tomato Vinaigrette and stir well.

5. Crumble the feta on the salad and stir gently to combine.

6. Serve immediately or refrigerate for up to 2 days.

7. If using pine nuts or almonds, add them just before serving.

NOTE: For best results, use sun-dried tomatoes packed in oil and preferably herbs. Buying them julienne-cut saves time. If you can find only halves in oil, chop them before adding them to the pasta.

DOUBLE UP!

Double up the Sun-Dried Tomato Vinaigrette (page 242) and use it in Marinated Chickpeas and Cucumbers (page 139).

Kimchi Quesadillas

WITH GREENS AND BEANS

These gooey, cheesy quesadillas need a mild, melty cheese, such as mozzarella, that puts the other flavors front and center—but Cheddar or Monterey Jack also work well. Don't discard the kimchi liquid, which, when whisked with sour cream or yogurt, makes a great dipping sauce.

SERVES 4   PREP: 10 MINUTES   COOK: 20 MINUTES   TOTAL: 30 MINUTES
cutting board • knife • large nonstick pan • medium mixing bowl • small bowl • hard spatula

---

5 ounces baby spinach (4 cups)

1 cup kimchi

1 tablespoon olive oil

one 15½-ounce can cannellini or great northern beans

10 ounces shredded mozzarella or mild cheese of choice

4 large tortillas, 9 inches in diameter

1 cup sour cream or plain yogurt

1 or 2 tablespoons pickling liquid from a jar of kimchi

1. Roughly chop the spinach. Finely chop the kimchi.

2. In a large nonstick pan over medium heat, heat the oil. Add the spinach and kimchi and cook, stirring occasionally, until the spinach wilts and the liquids evaporate, 3 to 5 minutes.

3. In a medium mixing bowl, combine the spinach, kimchi, beans, and mozzarella.

4. Wipe the nonstick pan and return it to medium heat.

5. Place a tortilla in the dry pan. Fill one side of the tortilla with one-quarter of the filling. Fold the tortilla over. If your pan has room for another quesadilla, repeat the process. Cook the quesadillas until golden brown on the outside and melty all the way through, 4 to 6 minutes total, flipping with a hard spatula halfway through cooking.

6. Repeat to cook all the quesadillas.

7. In a small bowl, whisk together the sour cream and the kimchi liquid, adjusting the ratio to taste.

8. Slice the quesadillas into wedges and serve with the sauce for dipping.

Kale and Ramen Salad

WITH SESAME GINGER VINAIGRETTE

Hearty kale and ginger vinaigrette meet the crunchy Midwestern Top Ramen salads of the 1990s. They all taste delicious, and they deserve to meet in one big bowl.

SERVES 4   PREP: 20 MINUTES   COOK: 10 MINUTES   TOTAL: 30 MINUTES
rimmed baking sheet · cutting board · knife · small bowl or jar · large salad bowl

½ cup slivered almonds

one 3-ounce package ramen noodles (seasoning packet discarded)

1 bunch (8 leaves) curly kale

6 green onions

1 batch Sesame Ginger Vinaigrette (page 243)

½ cup golden raisins

1½ cups shredded cooked chicken

VARIATION

To make it vegetarian, use shelled edamame instead of chicken.

1. Preheat the oven to 350°F.

2. On an unlined rimmed baking sheet, spread the slivered almonds. Crumble the dry noodles into small pieces (sometimes it's easiest to do this while the noodles are still inside the bag), some the size of the almonds and some twice as big. Bake until the almonds and noodles become toasted and golden, 10 to 12 minutes. Shake the pan halfway through cooking.

3. Meanwhile, stem the kale leaves and discard the stems. Finely chop the leaves and chop the green onions.

4. In a large salad bowl, combine the kale and the Sesame Ginger Vinaigrette. Use your hands to massage the vinaigrette gently into the kale so it softens and absorbs some of the liquid.

5. Stir in the green onions, golden raisins, and chicken.

6. Just before serving, stir in the toasted almonds and ramen noodles.

DOUBLE UP!

Make a double batch of Sesame Ginger Vinaigrette (page 243) and use it to make Cucumber Crunch Salad with Sesame Ginger Vinaigrette (page 135).

Chickpea Spinach Curry

This quick curry requires little prep and makes great leftovers. It uses red curry paste, common in Thai cooking, and curry powder, often used in Indian cuisines. The result doesn't fit authentically with either nation's traditions, but it absolutely teems with flavor and takes very little time.

SERVES 4   PREP: 5 MINUTES   COOK: 35 MINUTES   TOTAL: 40 MINUTES
medium saucepan or rice cooker • cutting board • knife • large skillet or Dutch oven

---

1½ cups uncooked white or brown rice

2 shallots

1½-inch piece fresh ginger, peeled

1 lime

two 15-ounce cans chickpeas

2 tablespoons cooking oil

2 tablespoons Thai-style red curry paste, more or less to taste

1 tablespoon mild curry powder

one 15 ½-ounce can coconut milk

2 tablespoons soy sauce

1½ teaspoons packed brown sugar

5 ounces baby spinach (4 cups)

plain yogurt or Miso Cashew Cream (page 9) for serving

1. On the stovetop or using a rice cooker, cook the rice according to package directions.

2. Dice the shallots and grate the ginger. Slice the lime into wedges. Drain and rinse the chickpeas.

3. In a large skillet or Dutch oven over medium heat, heat the cooking oil. Add the shallots and ginger and cook, stirring frequently, until fragrant, 2 to 3 minutes. Add the curry paste and curry powder and stir to combine.

4. Add the coconut milk, soy sauce, brown sugar, and chickpeas. When the liquid simmers, add the spinach and continue cooking, stirring often, until the spinach wilts and the sauce thickens and coats the chickpeas, 6 to 8 minutes.

5. Remove the curry from the heat. Squeeze half of the lime wedges into the dish.

6. Serve over rice with the remaining lime wedges on the side. Top with a spoonful of yogurt or Miso Cashew Cream.

NOTE: Don't use light coconut milk for this recipe. You need the full-fat kind.

Spinach and Shiitake Curry Ramen

If you have instant ramen in your pantry, here's a great way to liven it up. Instead of using the seasoning packets, make your own creamy, rich broth with coconut milk and Thai curry paste. Any color curry paste works, so use your favorite. The noodles and the spinach cook fast, so have your serving bowls ready to go.

SERVES 4   PREP: 15 MINUTES   COOK: 25 MINUTES   TOTAL: 40 MINUTES
small saucepan • cutting board • knife • large saucepan or wok

---

10 ounces shiitake mushrooms

5 ounces (4 cups) baby spinach

4 green onions

1 clove garlic

2 tablespoons cooking oil

3 tablespoons low-sodium soy sauce or tamari

two 15½-ounce cans coconut milk

2 to 4 tablespoons Thai red or green curry paste

4 cups low-sodium vegetable stock

2 tablespoons fish sauce

1 teaspoon brown sugar

4 eggs

1 lime

two 3-ounce packets instant ramen (seasoning packet discarded)

sesame seeds for garnish

sriracha or hot sauce of choice for serving (optional)

1. Fill a small saucepan half full with water. Bring it to a boil, then reduce the heat to low so it simmers until you're ready to use it.

2. While you wait for the water to boil, thinly slice the shiitake mushrooms. If the spinach leaves are large, roughly chop them. Thinly slice the green onions and mince the garlic.

3. In a large saucepan or wok over medium heat, heat the cooking oil. Add the mushrooms and cook, stirring occasionally, until they turn a deep golden brown, 5 to 7 minutes.

4. Add 1 tablespoon of the soy sauce and the garlic and cook for 1 more minute. Transfer the mushrooms to a bowl.

5. Return the pan to medium heat. Open one can of coconut milk. It should have a layer of thick coconut cream on top. Scoop 2 tablespoons of the cream into the pan. Add the curry paste and cook, stirring constantly, until fragrant, about 2 minutes.

6. Add the stock, all the remaining coconut milk (both cans), the remaining 2 tablespoons of soy sauce, the fish sauce, and brown sugar and simmer for 5 minutes.

7. Meanwhile, with a spoon, gently lower the eggs into the saucepan of simmering water. Cook for 7 minutes for room-temperature eggs or 8 minutes for refrigerated eggs.

CONTINUES →

8. Juice the lime for 1 tablespoon of fresh juice.

9. To the simmering ramen stock, add the noodles and spinach and cook just until the ramen becomes tender, 1 to 3 minutes. Stir in the lime juice.

10. Divide the stock and noodles among four serving bowls. Top each bowl with mushrooms.

11. Peel the eggs, slice them, and add them to the ramen.

12. Finish the bowls with the green onions, sesame seeds, and sriracha if desired.

NOTE: Don't use light coconut milk for this recipe. You need the full-fat kind.

VARIATION

To make it vegetarian, use low-sodium soy sauce or tamari instead of fish sauce.

Pizza Night

Pizza Veggie Board

Pizza night can fall short of serving up a rainbow. Use this board for inspiration to bring lots of veggies to the party. Make it as simple or as complex as you like: raw, lightly roasted, or fully cooked. Set the board out as a sampler for snacking while the pizza cooks. It skips the bread, cheese, and meat on most charcuterie boards because the pizza will have plenty of those!

SERVES 8 TO 10   PREP: 15 MINUTES   COOK: 10 MINUTES   TOTAL: 25 MINUTES
cutting board • knife • rimmed baking sheet • large board or platter for serving

½ medium head cauliflower or 6 ounces florets

1 bunch (6 ounces) broccolini

4 ounces green beans

1 bell pepper or 8 mini sweet bell peppers

2 carrots or 8 small rainbow carrots

1 tablespoon olive oil

1 teaspoon kosher salt

1 lemon

dips of choice

one 6-ounce bag roasted plantain chips

1. Preheat the oven to 450°F.

2. If using a head of cauliflower, chop it into florets. Halve store-bought florets. You should have about 2 cups.

3. Trim the ends of the broccolini and green beans. Slice the bell pepper in strips or halve the mini bell peppers lengthwise. Slice regular carrots into strips for dipping or halve rainbow carrots lengthwise.

4. Brush a rimmed baking sheet with the olive oil. Scatter the salt in the olive oil, distributing it evenly. Spread the broccolini, cauliflower, and green beans in a single layer on the prepared baking sheet. Bake the veggies, without disturbing, until they lightly brown on the bottom but still hold their shape and have some crunch, 6 to 8 minutes.

5. While the veggies roast, halve the lemon. When the veggies finish roasting, squeeze the lemon evenly over them. Let them cool on the sheet until cool enough to handle.

6. Arrange the veggie board by placing the dips in small bowls. Spread the vegetables and plantain chips around the dips.

NOTES: You can assemble the entire board and refrigerate it for up to 1 day in advance.

Look for lighter or plant-based dipping sauces to serve: Miso Cashew Cream (page 9), Green Goddess Sauce (page 245), baba ghanoush, hummus, spinach dip, or vegan ranch. The photo shows Trader Joe's Everything But the Bagel Dip and Chimichurri Sauce.

Pizza Salad
WITH PIZZA VINAIGRETTE

If you're not serving a Pizza Veggie Board (page 219), try adding this dish to your next pizza night. This salad gives classic red-sauce pizza vibes but with plenty of veggies in the mix. Chop and shred everything small so you can use your pizza crusts to scoop up the last bites.

SERVES 4 TO 6   PREP: 20 MINUTES   TOTAL: 20 MINUTES
cutting board · knife · large mixing or salad bowl · small bowl or jar

4 ounces seedless cucumber, such as English

1 cup cherry or grape tomatoes

2 hearts romaine lettuce

1 small head radicchio

one 2¼-ounce can sliced black olives

one 15½-ounce can chickpeas

1 ounce (½ cup) freshly grated Parmesan cheese

¼ small red onion

1 batch Pizza Vinaigrette (page 241)

1. Dice the cucumber and halve the tomatoes. Finely shred the romaine and radicchio. Drain the olives and chickpeas. Grate the Parmesan and dice the onion.

2. In a large mixing or salad bowl, combine all the ingredients that you just prepped.

3. Stir the salad and slowly add the Pizza Vinaigrette until dressed to taste. You may not need all of it.

VARIATION

To work another veggie into this dish, substitute 2 cups of baby spinach for 1 heart of romaine lettuce.

 TIP Not a fan of raw onion? Soak it in cold water first to minimize the bite or use Pickled Red Onions (page 245).

No-Fuss Pizza Crusts

After years of trying to find the best pizza dough for my family's Friday pizza nights, I decided to make my own. It took months of trial and error to get it right, but the result was worth it: a dough that requires no kneading, no appliances, and no messy flour-dusted counters. With this recipe, you're a few ingredients and minimal effort away from homemade pizza.

MAKES FOUR 10-INCH PIZZAS   PREP: 10 MINUTES, PLUS RISING TIME   COOK: 15 MINUTES
TOTAL: 1 HOUR 45 MINUTES
large mixing bowl • 2 rimmed baking sheets • parchment paper

---

4 cups (500 grams) all-purpose flour, plus more for dusting

one 2¼-teaspoon packet instant or fast-acting yeast

1½ teaspoons kosher salt

½ teaspoon sugar

1½ cups warm water, plus up to ¼ cup more if needed

olive oil for hands

toppings of choice

1. In a large mixing bowl, whisk together the flour, yeast, salt, and sugar.

2. Add the warm water and stir until the dough comes together in a sticky ball. If the dough seems dry and resists coming together, add up to ½ cup of additional warm water.

3. As you finish mixing, lightly grease one hand with some olive oil and use that hand to bring the dough together. You're not trying to knead it but to encourage it to form a sticky ball.

4. Cover the bowl with a clean dish towel and let it rise in a warm spot until it doubles in size, about 1 hour.

5. When the dough has doubled, line two baking sheets with parchment paper.

6. Generously dust the parchment and the surface of your pizza dough with flour.

7. Punch down the dough, then dust your hands with flour.

8. Quarter the dough and roll each quarter into a ball. Gently pull the sides down and tuck them under to form a relatively smooth surface. Place two balls on each prepared baking sheet.

9. If you have a pizza stone, put it in the oven and preheat the oven to 500°F. If you don't, arrange a rack in the lower position of the oven and another in the upper position and preheat it to 425°F.

CONTINUES →

10. Place the baking sheets, uncovered, near the oven while it heats, about 20 minutes.

11. On the parchment paper, use your fingers to stretch the dough into four circles, each 10 inches in diameter. If the dough resists spreading and springs back, let it rest at room temperature for 10 more minutes and try again.

12. Add toppings of choice.

13. Transfer the baking sheets to the oven or, if using a pizza stone, cut or tear each piece of parchment in half so each pizza sits on its own piece of parchment. Use a pizza peel to slide the parchment paper and pizzas onto the heated stone.

14. Bake until the pizza crusts turn golden, 10 to 12 minutes on a pizza stone or 14 to 16 minutes on a baking sheet.

15. Slice and serve.

NOTE: The water for the dough should feel warm, like a bath, but not hot.

These pizzas probably cook at a temperature higher than recommended for your parchment paper. A lot of research on using parchment paper at high temperatures has found it to be safe as long as the paper doesn't come in direct contact with the heat source. The paper will darken and crisp around the edges as it heats. To be extra safe, you can trim the parchment right to the edge of the dough, but I've been cooking pizza dough on parchment for more than a decade and never found it necessary.

TIP If you don't want to cook the dough right away, dust the dough balls with extra flour after step 8 and cover them tightly with plastic wrap. On baking sheets, refrigerate the dough for up to 2 days. The dough may need 10 to 20 minutes to come to room temperature before baking.

Brussels Sprouts and Pancetta Pizza

To make this pretty pizza, look for bags of shredded Brussels sprouts in the produce section of the grocery store. You *can* shred raw sprouts using the shredding blade of a food processor, but who wants to clean more dishes after pizza? Not me!

MAKES TWO 10-INCH PIZZAS   PREP: 10 MINUTES   COOK: 10 MINUTES   TOTAL: 20 MINUTES
large mixing bowl • box grater

8 ounces shredded Brussels sprouts

3 tablespoons olive oil

¼ teaspoon kosher salt

6 ounces low-moisture whole milk mozzarella

2 No-Fuss Pizza Crusts (page 223) or store-bought dough or crusts

4 ounces thinly sliced or diced pancetta

1. In a large mixing bowl, combine the Brussels sprouts with 1 tablespoon of the olive oil and the salt, stirring to coat evenly.

2. Into a bowl, grate the mozzarella.

3. Drizzle each round of crust with 1 tablespoon each of olive oil, followed by the mozzarella, Brussels sprouts, and pancetta. If using sliced pancetta, tear it into bite-size pieces first.

4. Cook as directed.

Farmers' Market Pesto Pizza

If you have access to a farmers' market full of fresh ingredients, just about any combination will make a great pizza. This one is my favorite.

MAKES TWO 10-INCH PIZZAS   PREP: 10 MINUTES   COOK: 10 MINUTES   TOTAL: 20 MINUTES
cutting board • knife • box grater

---

2 ears corn or 1¼ cups frozen corn kernels

10 cherry or grape tomatoes

4 ounces low-moisture whole milk mozzarella

¼ small red onion

2 No-Fuss Pizza Crusts (page 223) or store-bought dough or crusts

½ cup basil pesto

4 ounces goat cheese

fresh basil leaves for garnish

1. If using ears of corn, shuck and discard the husks. Lay the corn flat on a cutting board and slice off all the kernels. If using frozen, defrost it.

2. Halve the tomatoes, grate the mozzarella, and dice the onion.

3. Spread each round of crust with ¼ cup of pesto. Top it with the mozzarella, onion, tomatoes, and corn. Crumble the goat cheese evenly over the top. Cook as directed.

4. Top with fresh basil leaves.

Peanut Chicken Pizza

This pizza is a bit of a copycat version of a pizza on the menu of at least one popular American chain restaurant. I've lived in Thailand, so I'd like to say that I can resist the appeal of combining fresh, Thai-inspired flavors with bread and cheese, but something here just works. If you're a Thai-food purist, avert your eyes. But if a spicy, crunchy pizza with fresh herbs and a drizzle of sweet Thai chili dipping sauce instead of red sauce sounds good to you, you're going to love this one.

MAKES TWO 10-INCH PIZZAS PREP: 15 MINUTES COOK: 10 MINUTES TOTAL: 25 MINUTES
cutting board • knife • small and medium mixing bowls • box grater

---

⅔ cup roasted unsalted peanuts

6 ounces low-moisture whole milk mozzarella

¼ small red onion

3 cups shredded cooked chicken

3 tablespoons hoisin sauce

5 ounces shredded carrots

3 tablespoons olive oil

2 No-Fuss Pizza Crusts (page 223) or store-bought dough or crusts

sweet Thai chili dipping sauce

fresh cilantro

1. Roughly chop the peanuts, grate the mozzarella, and thinly slice the onion.

2. In a medium mixing bowl, combine the shredded chicken and hoisin sauce, stirring to coat lightly.

3. In a small mixing bowl, combine the carrots and onion with 1 tablespoon of the olive oil, stirring to coat evenly.

4. Drizzle each round of crust with 1 tablespoon each of olive oil and add the onions, carrots, and chicken. Top with the cheese and peanuts.

5. Cook as directed.

6. Finish the pizza with a generous drizzle of sweet Thai chili dipping sauce and tear the fresh cilantro leaves over the top.

Corn Chowder Pizza

Corn chowder tastes delicious, but you'll love it even more in pizza form. This pie makes the best of both worlds with thin-sliced potatoes, sweet corn, and crispy bacon in every bite.

MAKES TWO 10-INCH PIZZAS   PREP: 10 MINUTES   COOK: 25 MINUTES   TOTAL: 35 MINUTES
baking sheet · parchment paper · cutting board · knife · mandolin or sharp knife · box grater

---

8 strips bacon

3 ears corn or 2 cups frozen corn kernels

one 6-ounce russet potato

6 ounces Gruyère cheese

¼ bunch fresh chives, chopped

2 tablespoons olive oil

2 No-Fuss Pizza Crusts (page 223) or store-bought dough or crusts

¼ teaspoon red pepper flakes (optional)

1. Preheat the oven to 400°F.

2. Line a baking sheet with parchment paper. Spread the bacon on it in a single layer and bake, without disturbing, until crispy, 15 to 20 minutes.

3. Meanwhile, prepare the other toppings. If using ears of corn, shuck and discard the husks. Lay the corn flat on a cutting board and slice off all the kernels. If using frozen, defrost it.

4. Halve the potato lengthwise. With a mandolin or sharp knife, slowly and carefully slice the potato into discs about ¹⁄₁₆ inch thick.

5. Finely chop the chives and grate the cheese.

6. When the bacon has finished cooking, transfer it to a paper towel–lined plate to drain and cool.

7. Drizzle each round of crust with 1 tablespoon each of olive oil and add the potato slices in a single layer. Top evenly with the Gruyère and corn. Crumble the bacon over the top.

8. Cook as directed.

9. Top with the red pepper flakes, if using, and chopped chives.

Cauliflower Pistachio Pizza

When my taste testers sampled this unusual combination, they reported it was by far their favorite of all the recipes in this chapter. Double-roasting the cauliflower gives it a nutty, rich flavor. The idea to add pistachios came from a white pizza served at Tin Plate Pizza in Breckenridge, Colorado, and it's a game changer!

MAKES TWO 10-INCH PIZZAS   PREP: 10 MINUTES   COOK: 30 MINUTES   TOTAL: 40 MINUTES
cutting board • knife • rimmed baking sheet • box grater

---

1 medium head cauliflower (2 pounds or 12 ounces florets)

3 tablespoons olive oil

¼ teaspoon kosher salt

6 ounces low-moisture whole milk mozzarella

⅓ cup shelled pistachios

½ small red onion

2 No-Fuss Pizza Crusts (page 223) or store-bought dough or crusts

1. Preheat the oven to 425°F.

2. If using a head of cauliflower, chop it into florets. Halve store-bought florets. You should have about 4 cups.

3. Spread the florets out on a rimmed baking sheet. Drizzle them with 1 tablespoon of the olive oil and sprinkle with the salt. Stir gently to coat.

4. Roast the cauliflower on the upper rack until tender and golden in spots, 20 to 30 minutes, stirring halfway through cooking.

5. Meanwhile, grate the mozzarella, chop the pistachios, and thinly slice the onion.

6. When the cauliflower finishes cooking, roughly chop it into bite-size pieces.

7. Top each round of crust with 1 tablespoon of olive oil, the mozzarella, onions, cauliflower, and pistachios. Cook as directed.

Pizza Night

CHOOSE YOUR CRUST

No-Fuss Pizza
Crusts (page 223)

store-bought
dough or crusts

↓

GET SAUCY

marinara   pesto   olive oil

↓

CHOOSE YOUR CHEESE(S)

provolone   Parmesan   feta   Gruyère

mozzarella   Gorgonzola   goat cheese   ricotta

↓

ADD VEGETABLES

grated   roasted   roasted   mashed sweet
carrots   broccoli   cauliflower   potatoes

sliced or diced   sliced or   corn
bell peppers   diced zucchini   kernels

sliced   chopped   shredded   shredded
tomatoes   asparagus   Brussels sprouts   kale

baby   sliced
spinach leaves   mushrooms

Mix-and-Match

BOOST THE FLAVOR

pepperoncini   roasted or   olives   caramelized
sun-dried tomatoes   onions

sliced raw onions   roasted garlic   chopped nuts

PICK YOUR PROTEIN

Soyrizo or   hard-boiled   shredded rotisserie
meat substitutes   egg slices   chicken

cooked   cooked ground meat   cured
meatballs   or sausage   meats

FINISH IT
(AFTER COOKING)

baby arugula   pickled peppers   fresh herbs

hot honey   dried spice blends

Sauces, Dressings, and Extras

These subrecipes make veggie dishes shine. Double the batches—or more if you're feeling adventurous!—to use in more than one recipe.

Dry Rub

A jar of this all-purpose spice blend comes in handy when you don't have a plan but need to flavor proteins or vegetables before cooking. It goes with almost anything. It nicely spices Salmon Tacos with Corn and Avocado Salsa (page 128) and Dry-Rub Chicken with Cucumber Peach Salsa (page 136), or you can add it to 1 pound of protein or vegetable of your choice.

MAKES 4 TEASPOONS   PREP: 5 MINUTES   TOTAL: 5 MINUTES
mixing bowl • spoon

1 teaspoon kosher salt

1 teaspoon ground cumin

1 teaspoon chili powder

¼ teaspoon garlic powder

¼ teaspoon brown sugar

black pepper

In a small bowl, combine all the ingredients. Store in an airtight container at room temperature for up to 3 months.

Gochujang Yogurt Sauce

This recipe adds creamy heat to Sweet Potatoes, Broccoli, and Gochujang Chicken (page 61), No-Roll Sushi Bowls (page 143), Banh Mi Bowls with Quick-Pickled Carrots (page 25), and Green Bean and Ginger Wraps with Chicken (page 172). (Banh Mi Bowls use sriracha for spice, but gochujang works just fine.) Be sure to use Korean gochujang sauce—smoky, spicy, and subtly sweet—that usually contains vinegar, sesame oil, soy sauce, and a sweetener added to a gochujang paste (just fermented spicy red peppers). You should be able to find the sauce in the international or Asian section of a grocery store.

MAKES ABOUT 1 CUP   PREP: 5 MINUTES   TOTAL: 5 MINUTES
small bowl • whisk

1 cup plain yogurt

2 tablespoons mayonnaise

1 to 4 tablespoons gochujang sauce

In a small bowl, whisk together all the ingredients. Refrigerate until the use-by date on the yogurt.

NOTE: Start with 1 tablespoon of gochujang sauce, taste, and slowly increase the measure to your preferred spice level.

Maple Tahini Dressing

This recipe adds savory sweetness to Roasted Carrot and Orzo Salad (page 15) and Pita Crunch Salad with Roasted Brussels Sprouts (page 200).

MAKES 1 CUP   PREP: 5 MINUTES   TOTAL: 5 MINUTES
small bowl • whisk

¼ cup apple cider vinegar

3 tablespoons tahini

2 teaspoons maple syrup

½ teaspoon kosher salt

½ cup olive oil

1. In a small bowl, whisk together the vinegar, tahini, maple syrup, and salt.

2. While whisking, add the olive oil.

3. Refrigerate for up to 1 week. It will thicken when cold, so let it come to room temperature and stir well before using.

Pizza Vinaigrette

This tangy dressing gives classic pizza vibes in the best way. It brings tart, herby flavor to Greek Salad Jars with Quinoa (page 140) and Pizza Salad (page 220), or you can toss it with any crisp greens and veggies in your fridge.

MAKES ¾ CUP   PREP: 5 MINUTES   TOTAL: 5 MINUTES
cutting board • knife • small bowl or jar • whisk

1 clove garlic

¼ cup red wine vinegar

2 teaspoons honey

1 teaspoon Dijon mustard

½ teaspoon dried oregano

¼ teaspoon kosher salt

½ cup olive oil

1. Mince or grate the garlic.

2. In a small bowl or jar, whisk or shake together the garlic, vinegar, honey, mustard, oregano, and salt. If using a bowl, slowly add the olive oil while whisking. If using a jar, add the olive oil and shake again until smooth.

3. Refrigerate for up to 1 week. It will thicken when cold, so let it come to room temperature and stir well before using.

Balsamic Vinaigrette

Pair any salad greens with this vinaigrette and you have a side dish for almost any meal. This recipe adds savory tang to Sweet Potato Cobb Salad (page 55) and Farro Caprese (page 150).

MAKES ¾ CUP   PREP: 10 MINUTES   TOTAL: 10 MINUTES
knifecutting board · small bowl or jar · whisk

1 shallot

¼ cup balsamic vinegar

1 teaspoon Dijon mustard

1 teaspoon honey

¼ teaspoon kosher salt

½ cup olive oil

1. Mince the shallot. You should have about 2 teaspoons.

2. In a small bowl or jar, whisk or shake together the shallot, balsamic vinegar, mustard, honey, and salt. If using a bowl, slowly add the olive oil while whisking. If using a jar, add the oil and shake again until smooth.

3. Refrigerate for up to 1 week. It will thicken when cold, so let it come to room temperature and stir well before using.

 TIP Balsamic vinegar can vary in sweetness, depending on brand and age. If you're using a tart and tangy vinegar, add some more honey for balance. Taste the vinaigrette and adjust until you achieve the right balance of sweet and tart.

Sun-Dried Tomato Vinaigrette

Sun-dried tomatoes can add a taste of summer at any time of year. They bring a sweet, savory taste to Marinated Chickpeas and Cucumbers (page 139) and Pearl Couscous Salad (page 206). This vinaigrette also works great as a dressing for any pasta salad.

MAKES ¾ CUP   PREP: 10 MINUTES   TOTAL: 10 MINUTES
cutting board · knife · small bowl · whisk

½ cup sun-dried tomatoes in oil with herbs

1 shallot

¼ cup balsamic vinegar

¼ teaspoon kosher salt

¼ cup olive oil (or use the oil from the jar of sun-dried tomatoes)

1. Mince the tomatoes and shallot.

2. In a small bowl, whisk together the sun-dried tomatoes, shallot, balsamic vinegar, and salt. While whisking, slowly add the olive oil.

3. Refrigerate for up to 1 week. It will thicken when cold, so let it come to room temperature and stir well before using.

Sesame Ginger Vinaigrette

This recipe adds savory bite to Cucumber Crunch Salad (page 135) and Kale and Ramen Salad (page 210).

MAKES ⅔ CUP   PREP: 10 MINUTES   TOTAL: 10 MINUTES
cutting board • knife • grater • small bowl or jar

1-inch piece fresh ginger, peeled

¼ cup cooking oil

2 tablespoons low-sodium soy sauce or tamari

2 tablespoons rice vinegar

2 teaspoons toasted sesame oil

2 teaspoons honey

1 teaspoon white sesame seeds

¼ teaspoon kosher salt

1. Grate the ginger.

2. In a small bowl or jar, whisk or shake together all the ingredients.

3. Refrigerate for up to a week.

Peanut Sauce

This sauce can transform a meal from ordinary to exciting. It barely even needs a plan. Drizzle it on salads, grilled meats, or noodles—or dip veggies in it. It also adds creamy texture and rich flavor to Peanut Noodles with Green Beans (page 168) and Asparagus Summer Rolls (page 185). Use warm water to help the ingredients mix together easily. The sauce may seem slightly thin but will thicken as it cools.

MAKES 1⅓ CUPS   PREP: 15 MINUTES   TOTAL: 15 MINUTES
cutting board • knife • grater • small bowl • whisk

1½-inch piece fresh ginger

½ cup creamy peanut butter

⅓ cup warm water

¼ cup low-sodium soy sauce or tamari

1 tablespoon rice vinegar

1 tablespoon honey

1 teaspoon toasted sesame oil

1 teaspoon chili garlic sauce or sriracha

1. Peel and grate the ginger.

2. Whisk together the peanut butter, warm water, soy sauce, vinegar, ginger, honey, sesame oil, and chili garlic sauce until smooth.

3. The sauce may seem thin if it is still warm from the water, but it will thicken up as it cools.

4. Refrigerate for up to 1 week. Let it come to room temperature and stir well before using.

NOTE: This recipe uses conventional creamy peanut butter, which contains salt and a little sugar. If using unsalted or natural peanut butter, taste the sauce and add salt or more honey if needed.

Green Goddess Sauce

This recipe adds herby goodness to Zucchini and Corn Tostadas (page 111), Green Goddess Grain Bowls with Asparagus and Chicken (page 183), and BLAT Salad (page 152). The herbs will release moisture, producing a thick, pourable sauce. If it seems too thick, add a splash of water.

MAKES 1½ CUPS PREP: 15 MINUTES TOTAL: 15 MINUTES
cutting board • knife • blender or food processor

1 large lemon

4 cups loosely packed fresh herbs, such as basil, chives, cilantro, green onions, parsley, etc.

1 cup plain yogurt

½ cup olive oil

¼ cup mayonnaise

1 clove garlic

½ teaspoon kosher salt

1. Juice the lemon for 2 tablespoons of fresh juice.

2. In a blender or food processor, combine all the ingredients and blend or process until smooth.

3. Refrigerate for up to 3 days.

> **VARIATION**
>
> To make it vegan, add the herbs, garlic, and 2 tablespoons of fresh lemon juice to a batch of Miso Cashew Cream (page 9).

Pickled Red Onions

This recipe adds tangy, zesty magic to Green Goddess Grain Bowls with Asparagus and Chicken (page 183) and Sweet Potato Cobb Salad (page 55).

MAKES 2 CUPS PREP: 10 MINUTES, PLUS MARINATING TIME TOTAL: 30 MINUTES
small bowl • whisk • cutting board • knife • 16-ounce jar

½ cup hot water

1½ tablespoons sugar or honey

2 teaspoons kosher salt

½ cup apple cider vinegar

1 small red onion

1. Fill a small bowl with the hot water. Whisk in the sugar and salt until dissolved.

2. Whisk in the vinegar.

3. Let the liquids cool slightly while you thinly slice the onion and pack it tightly into a 16-ounce jar.

4. Pour the pickling liquid over the onion and seal the jar.

5. Let the pickles soak at room temperature for at least 20 minutes or refrigerate for up to 2 weeks.

 TIP Repurpose the leftover pickling liquid by using it instead of the vinegar in any vinaigrette. Skip any added sweetener or salt, as the pickling liquid already includes those elements.

No-Knead Focaccia

This simple and surprisingly satisfying bread goes great with soup, such as Red Lentil and Sweet Potato Soup with Cumin (page 51) or Red Pepper Soup with Roasted Chickpeas (page 92), and it frames amazing sandwiches, such as Stuffed Focaccia with Zucchini and Pesto Mayo (page 106). If you like thick-crust pizza, use it for any of the pizza recipes in the Pizza Night chapter (pages 217–237). Even if you've never made bread before, you'll love the results.

SERVES 6 TO 8   PREP: 10 MINUTES, PLUS RISING TIME   COOK: 24 MINUTES
TOTAL: 2 HOURS 30 MINUTES
large mixing bowl • 9-by-13-inch baking pan • parchment paper

---

4 cups (500 g) all-purpose flour

2 teaspoons kosher salt

1 tablespoon sugar

1 packet (2¼ teaspoons) fast-acting or instant yeast

2 cups warm water

¼ cup olive oil

1 teaspoon sea salt flakes, such as Maldon

1. In a large mixing bowl, whisk together the flour, kosher salt, sugar, and yeast.

2. Add the water and stir until no dry spots remain. Scrape down the sides as you stir. The dough will feel sticky and wet like thick pancake batter.

3. Cover the bowl with a clean dish towel and let it rise on the kitchen counter until it doubles in size, about 1 hour.

4. To make it easy to remove the bread from the pan, line a 9-by-13-inch baking dish with a piece of parchment paper so that the edges hang over the longer sides.

5. Pour 1 tablespoon of the olive oil on the parchment paper and tip it around to coat the parchment paper and any exposed parts of the pan. Transfer the dough into the prepared pan. Lightly grease your hands with olive oil and flatten the dough, pressing it uniformly to the edges of the pan.

6. Place the dough, uncovered, in a warm location in your kitchen and let it rise again until puffy and 50 percent bigger, about 1 more hour.

7. When the dough is about halfway through its second rise, position a rack in the center of the oven and preheat it to 450°F.

8. When the dough has finished rising, lightly oil your fingers and poke through the dough until your fingers touch the parchment paper.

CONTINUES →

9. Drizzle the remaining 3 tablespoons of olive oil on the focaccia and sprinkle with sea salt flakes.

10. Bake until the top turns golden brown, 24 to 28 minutes. If you have an instant-read thermometer, the bread is done when it reaches 190°F in the center.

11. Let the bread cool in the pan for 5 minutes, then turn it out on a cooling rack to cool completely to room temperature before slicing.

 TIP If your kitchen runs on the colder side, the dough may need 75 minutes to rise (step 3) and another 75 minutes to proof (step 6).

Meal Plans

Put my six tips for How to Meal Plan Like a Pro (page xiv) into action. The plans on the following pages use these tips to help you save time and money.

1. **DOUBLE UP.** Each plan lists what you can prep or cook once and use twice.
2. **PREP AHEAD.** Proper prior planning always makes cooking easier.
3. **BUY ONE HERB.** These plans highlight which herb you can incorporate into the week and, in some cases, additional ways to use it.
4. **COOK PERISHABLES FIRST.** In the plans, you'll make fish, uncured meat, and similar items early in the week.
5. **PLAN EASY WINS.** Make adjustments to fit your schedule. Swap in an easy, go-to meal and/or take a night off.

To make any of these plans in their entirety, follow the QR code for a ready-made grocery list.

BUSY WEEK

Whether you're going to have an action-packed week or you just want more time to relax in the evenings, this plan features quick and easy meals.

Double Up:
- Green onions (W, F)
- Fresh or frozen corn (W, Th)

Prep Ahead:
- Dice ham and bell peppers (M)
- Chop cauliflower florets (F)

 HERB TIP   Use a bunch of basil in Thai Broccoli Slaw (T) and One-Pan Orzo (Th).

MONDAY	TUESDAY	WEDNESDAY	THURSDAY	FRIDAY	SHOPPING LIST
Denver Omelet Wrap (page 83)	Thai Broccoli Slaw (page 34) + roasted or grilled sausages	Miso Butter Soba Noodles with Corn and Chicken (page 118)	One-Pan Orzo with Tomatoes, Corn, and Feta (page 149)	Kung Pao Cauliflower (page 74)	

SPRING FLING

When the days get warmer and you're craving something fresh that you can enjoy outdoors, these meals will hit the spot.

Double Up:
- Baby arugula (M, W)

Prep Ahead:
- Cook quinoa (W)

Double Up and Prep Ahead:
- Trim asparagus (M, T)
- Make Peanut Sauce (page 244; T, Th)

 HERB TIP   Use fresh basil in Picnic Sandwiches (M) and Asparagus Summer Rolls (T). Save a handful of leaves to top Friday's pizza.

MONDAY	TUESDAY	WEDNESDAY	THURSDAY	FRIDAY	SHOPPING LIST
Picnic Sandwiches with Basil Dijonnaise (page 180)	Asparagus Summer Rolls with Peanut Sauce (page 185)	Black Bean Smash Burgers (page 97)	Peanut Noodles with Green Beans (page 168)	Farmers' Market Pesto Pizza (page 228)	

SUMMER LOVIN'

If it's hot outside, make these meals. They require minimal time in front of the stove or oven and showcase summer's bounty of produce.

Double Up and Prep Ahead:

- Cook farro (M, Th)
- Make Green Goddess Sauce (page 245; M, W)

Prep Ahead:

- Make Pickled Red Onions (page 245; M)
- Make Balsamic Vinaigrette (page 242; Th)

 HERB TIP If you have a basil plant or buy a bunch of it at the store, this is the week to use it because you can use it in all of this week's meals.

MONDAY	TUESDAY	WEDNESDAY	THURSDAY	FRIDAY	SHOPPING LIST
Green Goddess Grain Bowls with Asparagus and Chicken (page 183)	Harissa Gazpacho (page 160) + Dry-Rub Chicken with Cucumber Peach Salsa (page 136)	Zucchini and Corn Tostadas with Green Goddess Sauce (page 111)	Farro Caprese (page 150) + grilled protein of your choice	Summer Squash Toast with Goat Cheese (page 101)	

SWEATER WEATHER

If it's chilly outside, these meals will warm you up.

Double Up and Prep Ahead:

- Peel and slice carrots (M, Th)
- Chop cauliflower florets (W, F)
- Make Maple Tahini Dressing (page 241; M, W)

Prep Ahead:

- Roast Brussels sprouts and toast pita bread (W)

 HERB TIP Use fresh parsley in Salerno Spaghetti (T) and Roasted Cauliflower and Tahini Soup (W). If you have any leftover parsley, chop it up and top Thursday's risotto and/or Friday's pizza with it.

MONDAY	TUESDAY	WEDNESDAY	THURSDAY	FRIDAY	SHOPPING LIST
Roasted Carrot and Orzo Salad with Maple Tahini Dressing (page 15)	Salerno Spaghetti with Broccolini (page 41)	Roasted Cauliflower and Tahini Soup (page 69) + Pita Crunch Salad with Roasted Brussels Sprouts (page 15)	Curried Carrot Risotto with Crispy Shiitakes (page 27)	Cauliflower Pistachio Pizza (page 235)	

Build a Bowl

Bowl meals easily allow you to combine ingredients that wouldn't come together well on a plate. Use this guide to build a bowl of your favorites or create new combinations.

START WITH A VEGETABLE

ROAST carrots, broccoli, sweet potatoes, cauliflower, asparagus, Brussels sprouts

CHOP cucumbers, tomatoes, kale, spinach

SAUTÉ bell peppers, zucchini, corn, green beans

CHOOSE A BASE

grains   greens

ADD A PROTEIN

Pan-Fried Tofu
(page 5)

Red Lentil Bites
(page 13)

Roasted Chickpeas
(page 6)

chopped deli meat   rotisserie chicken

GET SAUCY

Miso Cashew Cream
(page 9)

Gochujang Yogurt Sauce
(page 240)

Maple Tahini Dressing
(page 241)

Pizza Vinaigrette
(page 241)

Balsamic Vinaigrette
(page 242)

Sun-Dried Tomato
Vinaigrette (page 242)

Sesame Ginger Vinaigrette
(page 243)

Green Goddess Sauce
(page 245)

Peanut Sauce (page 244)

↓

ADD CRUNCH

Hot Honey Granola
(page 10)

croutons

crispy wontons

tortilla or pita chips

toasted or raw nuts

↓

ADD EXTRAS

Pickled Red
Onions
(page 245)

fresh herbs

avocado

cheese

No-Recipe Meals

Maybe you planned meals for the week, or maybe you winged it each night. If you cooked, chances look good that you have a fridge full of random bits and pieces. Here's how you might use some of those random ingredients. Never underestimate the power of a delicious sauce to bring everything together.

START WITH A VEGETABLE

| asparagus | bell peppers | broccoli | Brussels sprouts |
| carrots | cauliflower | squash | zucchini |

↓

COOK IT

roasted   sautéed   steamed

↓

ADD A STARCH

bread or rolls

bulgur, farro,
quinoa, rice

pasta

rice

tortillas

PACK IT WITH PROTEIN		GET SAUCY		ADD SOME EXTRAS		FINISHED MEAL
Roasted Chickpeas (page 6)	+	mashed avocado	+	red pepper flakes or chili powder	=	loaded avocado toast
cheese	+	Miso Cashew Cream (page 9)	+	a handful of baby spinach or arugula	=	veggie sandwiches
Hot Honey Granola (page 10)	+	Green Goddess Sauce (page 245) or Maple Tahini Dressing (page 241)	+	extra greens, lettuce, or herbs	=	grain bowls
white beans	+	marinara	+	cheese	=	veggie pasta bake
fried egg	+	Gochujang Yogurt Sauce (page 240)	+	kimchi	=	bibimbap
Pan-Fried Tofu (page 5)	+	Gochujang Yogurt Sauce (page 240)	+	seaweed snacks or nori sheets, fried onions or shallots	=	sushi bowls
beans, black or refried	+	salsa	+	sliced avocado and cilantro	=	veggie tacos

Acknowledgments

This book wouldn't have been possible without the careful review, thoughtful feedback, and many photos of a team of recipe testers. So much gratitude goes to Audra Clark, who has reviewed my writing from those AP English essays in high school and who is still my best proofreader, tester, and friend. We logged thousands of steps during the creation of this book, and I truly couldn't have done it without your honest feedback, your hours in the kitchen testing these recipes, and your unwavering support. And to Bryan, Addie, Kaya, and Macy for your irreplaceable role as tasters in the test kitchen.

My amazing team of volunteer recipe testers, your generosity in letting these recipes have a place at your dinner tables before they went into the world overwhelmed me. Huge thanks to Erika Barber, Mayan Barkel, Shannon Barna, Susie Bradford, Molly Buchanan, Karen Clark, Joy Clarke, Gina Dickson, Franci Erdmann, Rachel Flaster, Andrea Garcia, Erin Gierhart, Lauren Gniazdowski, Cindy and Helen Jones, Susan LeBailly, Suzanne Marty, Nicole Mink, Beth Mitchell, Kari Mitchell, Sarah Niehoff, Jean Olson, Meaghan O'Shea, Aubree Shay, Lisa Shay, Michael Shay, Patrick Shay, Kate Shungu, Shanna Smith, Alyssa and Brian Thomas, the Tragert Family, Elizabeth Villarroel and Jack Vessey, Jennifer Vitela, Lynn Watkins, Shannon Witcher, and Jen Wooster.

My parents planted the seed of my curiosity in the kitchen when I was young. Mom, thank you for your encouragement to chase my dreams from the very beginning, for lunches and phone calls so I could vent and dream, and for being the type of parent who spends 48 hours laminating dough for the most spectacular Christmas morning pastry. Dad, thank you for passing on the creative bug, cooking delicious dinners day in and day out, and packing lunches for a semi-vegetarian teenager who preferred caprese sandwiches over PB&Js. To my bonus parent, Kirk, for your genuine interest in and support of this project and all my work; and to my brother, Jono, who was right there next to me at every family dinner and who I'm grateful to have as a friend in adulthood.

Veronica, Rachel, and Banti, thank you for serving as hand models throughout these pages and for putting up with me when I was in full, intense work mode. Veronica and Rachel, thank you for jumping in to work with me through photo shoots and to complete the myriad, random tasks that take place in my kitchen on workdays, and for washing hundreds (thousands?) of dishes with me. I'm so lucky to have you three as my sisters.

This entire journey started on a call with Dianne Jacob, who gave me the honest feedback that I needed in the earliest days of this book. Thank you, Dianne, for believing in it when it was just an idea that I hadn't even put on paper and for coaching me through the process of bringing it to life.

Enormous thanks to my talented agent, Marilyn Allen, for making all this happen and for cheering me on at every step. I'm so glad to have you in my corner.

Thank you to the entire team at Countryman Press, for taking my words and images and transforming them into this beautiful book. In particular, thank you to my editor, James Jayo, for your incredible editing skills and insightful feedback, and to Allison Chi, for your artistic vision. Thank you also to Ann Treistman, Jess Murphy, Devon Zahn, Zach Polendo, and Devorah Backman, and to freelance indexer Barbara Mortenson for a last-minute catch.

To Anna Petrow, the biggest thanks for lending your incredible talents to this project. Your guidance on the photography, keen styling skills, and sense of fun about it all made my shoot days with you my favorites.

To the talented women of my Masterminds—Kari Anderson, Gina Dickson, Erin Gierhart, Katy McAvoy, and Jen Wooster and Sarah Cook, Amanda Gajdosik, Emmeline Kemperyd, Kylie Lato, Jennifer Pallian, Amanda Scarlati, and Katie Trant—you took this lonely business of food writing and made it a thriving community. I can't remember what I did before I had your daily dose of rants and laughs.

I have the best friends a girl could ever ask for. Joanna Shearon, Susie Bradford, Lindsay Buhs, and Kelsey Ragsdale, thank you for the walks, motivating texts, dinners to escape the mess of my kitchen, and letting me hash things out over many cups of coffee and glasses of wine.

To Karen Warden and Audra Clark, my longest friends and cheerleaders, for being a sounding board in recent years and all the years before them. Thank you for testing and rating all my pizzas so that we could put the very best in this book. To all the fourth graders out there, be on the lookout! The friends you make now may be your best friends forever.

To Lisa Coleman, I'm grateful every day that we connected and get to work together. But I'm especially grateful for your friendship and collaboration on the hectic days when it's just the two of us keeping the wheels of this small business turning. Sophie Sadler, it's rare to find someone who understands this strange career and even rarer to find someone who then becomes a dear friend. Thank you for cheering me on at the exact right moments when I wanted to throw in the towel.

A very special thank-you to my Cook Smarts colleagues and community of home cooks who shaped how I think about getting creative dinners on the table in a reasonable amount of time. Special thanks to my dear friend and fellow foodie Sarah Byun, and to Jess Dang, for believing in me and my work from the very beginning and for showing me that it's possible to make a living doing what you love.

Frank, you are my favorite person. Thank you for helping me to dream big and for your unwavering support as I chase those dreams. You bring so much joy into my life and into our home, and there's still no one in the world I'd rather hang out with. I'm so glad that you emailed me before I got on that train to Bulgaria.

Molly, Clara, and June, you changed my life for the better when you made me a mom. Thank you for coming to a dinner table piled high with vegetables night after night in (mostly) good spirits. Never forget how much cauliflower we ate this year. This really is all for you.

Balsamic Goddess Gochujang Peanut Sauce Pizza

Index